Research in Contemporary Religion

Edited by
Carla Danani, Judith Gruber, Hans-Günter Heimbrock,
Stefanie Knauss, Daria Pezzoli-Olgiati,
Else Marie Wiberg Pedersen, Hans-Joachim Sander,
Trygve Wyller

In co-operation with
Hanan Alexander (Haifa), Wanda Deifelt (Decorah),
Siebren Miedema (Amsterdam), Bonnie J. Miller-McLemore
(Nashville), Garbi Schmidt (Roskilde), Claire Wolfteich (Boston)

Volume 35

Vandenhoeck & Ruprecht

Tarald Rasmussen / Vegard Ree Ytterbøe (eds.)

Protestantism and Protestantization

Vandenhoeck & Ruprecht

Bibliographic information published by the Deutsche Nationalbibliothek
The Deutsche Nationalbibliothek lists this publication in the Deutsche Nationalbibliografie;
detailed bibliographic data available online: https://dnb.de.

© 2023 by Vandenhoeck & Ruprecht, Theaterstraße 13, 37073 Göttingen, Germany,
an imprint of the Brill-Group
(Koninklijke Brill NV, Leiden, The Netherlands; Brill USA Inc., Boston MA, USA;
Brill Asia Pte Ltd, Singapore; Brill Deutschland GmbH, Paderborn, Germany;
Brill Österreich GmbH, Vienna, Austria)
Koninklijke Brill NV incorporates the imprints Brill, Brill Nijhoff, Brill Hotei,
Brill Schöningh, Brill Fink, Brill mentis, Vandenhoeck & Ruprecht, Böhlau,
V&R unipress and Wageningen Academic.

All rights reserved. No part of this work may be reproduced or utilized in any form or by any
means, electronic or mechanical, including photocopying, recording, or any information
storage and retrieval system, without prior written permission from the publisher.

Cover design: SchwabScantechnik, Göttingen
Typesetting: le-tex publishing services, Leipzig
Printed and bound: Hubert & Co. BuchPartner, Göttingen
Printed in the EU

Vandenhoeck & Ruprecht Verlage | www.vandenhoeck-ruprecht-verlage.com

ISSN 2198-7556
ISBN 978-3-525-56872-9

Table of Contents

Tarald Rasmussen, Vegard Ree Ytterbøe
Preface 7

Tarald Rasmussen
Chapter 1: Protestantism and Protestantisation. An Introduction 9

Oddbjørn Leirvik
Chapter 2: Protestantisation of Islam – as Good, Humanistic Religion 17

Gina Lende
Chapter 3: The Protestant Newcomer. Politics, Economics and
Pentecostal Growth 31

Karin Neutel
Chapter 4: Requiring Religious Motivations. Reflections on the
Norwegian Law on Circumcision 51

Vebjørn L. Horsfjord
Chapter 5: Protestantisations in the Norwegian Debate on Circumcision 67

Erlend From
Chapter 6: None of the Above. Yet a Tad Protestant? 83

Trygve Wyller
Chapter 7: Can Protestants Resist Christianism? Scandinavian
Creation Theology As Political Theology 111

Allen G Jorgenson
Chapter 8: Sensual Protestations: Luther, Løgstrup and the Promise
of the Senses 121

Index 135

Notes on Contributors 137

Tarald Rasmussen, Vegard Ree Ytterbøe

Preface

The present volume has been developed from the research project "Good Protestant – Bad Religion" funded by the Norwegian Research Council.[1] The project itself as well as several contributions in this volume has a focus on the case of Norway. At the same time, it has been essential to make the case studies relevant and significant within a broader religious studies discussion.

Researchers from different fields of the broad religious studies landscape – including theology – have contributed in the project, and also in this volume. An important initiator of the project and a key researcher within it was Helge Aarsheim. Vegard Ree Ytterbøe has – together with the project leader Tarald Rasmussen – had an essential role in the management of the project and is also the coeditor of this volume.

---

1 https://www.tf.uio.no/english/research/projects/goba/index.html.

Tarald Rasmussen

Chapter 1: Protestantism and Protestantisation. An Introduction

Historically, the concept of "Protestantism" has been used in quite different ways. In the social sciences, debates on Protestantism have been strongly influenced by Max Weber and his studies of the relationship between Protestant ethics and the development of capitalism.[1] Here, Protestantism has primarily been defined by focusing on a special kind of ethics. This Weberian approach has also had considerable impact on the connotations of the "Protestantism" concept in the broader public debate.

In theology, philosophy and religious studies, other approaches to the concept have dominated. Here, the Protestant belief system and its focus on religious subjectivity have been major concerns, and discussions throughout the post-Reformation centuries have often been linked to the relationship between Protestantism and (Western) modernity.[2]

An archaeology of Protestantism

A brief look back to recent research on the history of Protestantism can help to broaden and differentiate both the Weberian and the traditional theological approaches. The Lutheran and Calvinist Reformations in the sixteenth century were the starting point of fundamental transformations of Christianity. In Reformation research, these transformations have frequently been labelled a "confessionalization" of the Christian religion.[3] The Roman Catholic Church did not succeed in suppressing the Lutheran and the Calvinist traditions as heresies. Instead, the two new parties succeeded in establishing themselves as legitimate confessions. The Lutheran confession was legally acknowledged at the Diet in Augsburg in 1555. The Calvinist or Reformed confession was also a tempting alternative to several

---

1 An extensive and updated bibliography on discussions of the "Weberian thesis" within sociology and the social sciences can be found in Käsler (2014), 969–971.
2 Interesting contributions to this debate can be found in von Scheliha and Schröder (Ed.) (1998).
3 An overview of the early modern confessionalization of Christianity is available in Ehrenpreis and Lotz-Heumann (2002).

European Princes during the latter half of the sixteenth century, but was not acknowledged as a legitimate confession in the German Empire until 1648, after the war in Europe.

Along with the emerging new confessions, Catholic Christianity also underwent a fundamental change and had to reinvent itself according to the structural patterns of the confessionalization (Reinhard and Schilling, 1995). This transformation had a major turning point at the council of Trent 1545–63, and was followed up by the papacy well into the seventeenth century.

Together, the two anti-Roman confessional parties: the Lutherans and the Calvinists, were acknowledged as the *Protestants*. They had both departed from the Catholic Church for similar reasons:

1. A protest against the hierarchy. Christian truth has to be found by reading the Bible, not by appealing to the pope.
2. An urgent need to promote the religious authority of the individual: Christianity is most of all a matter of individual faith, and not a matter of celebrations and rituals depending on a separate clergy class.
3. After departing from the authority of Rome: A pursuit of new ways of relating religion to politics, with support either from city councils or from Protestant princes. These main characteristics were typical of the sixteenth and seventeenth centuries. During the eighteenth and nineteenth centuries, new varieties of Protestantism emerged, including the denominations of Methodism, Baptism and Pentecostalism. They all shared the initial key ideas of early modern Protestants, but were at the same time intent on promoting the religious individual in new ways. Two shared characteristics are:
4. An increasing appeal to the spiritual experience of the individual, and
5. Loosening or totally removing the links between religious affiliation and a particular territory. Departing from the supportive political contexts (city councils or princes) of early modern Protestantism, the new denominations preferred to organize themselves at a distance from the political sphere, and without an institutional connection to a specific territory.

At first glance, this seems like a history of gradual development of Protestant ideals. However, an "archaeology of Protestantism" has to pay attention to the fact that all these five characteristics are still also relevant for describing the present situation. At least one could say that the traditional links between territory and confession are still relevant in some parts of Protestantism. In countries like Norway, and even more so Denmark, national legislation still gives certain priorities to the Protestant religion. On the other hand: Protestantism without territorial links also existed in the sixteenth century with the Anabaptist movement, persecuted by all legal confessions but still able to establish networks across Europe.

Three core dimensions of Protestantism

A. *FREEDOM.* This was a key concept in all main Protestant traditions, among Lutherans, Reformed and Anabaptists, as well as in a number of classical texts of early modern Protestantism. Protestant ideals of freedom were promoted on an individual as well as on a societal level, with the individual freedom of the believer as the fundamental value. But in order to promote the individual freedom of the believer, it was necessary to be liberated from the legal and political captivities the Christians were held in by the Roman Church.

B. *NORMATIVE CENTRATION.* The German church historian Berndt Hamm has suggested the key concept "normative Zentrierung" as a fundamental structural characteristic of the Protestant movement (Hamm, 1992). All main Protestant traditions agreed that they had to shed and leave behind superfluous parts of Catholic religion and concentrate on the essentials – even if these essentials were defined somewhat differently by different parts of the Protestant tradition. However, they all agreed on the necessity of a) Reducing ritual expressions, b) Minimizing and concentrating on clerical functions, c) Promoting the Bible as normative source.

C. *NO SEPARATE SPHERE OF RELIGIOUS LEGISLATION.* In a legal context, the Lutheran and Calvinist traditions are characterized by a protest against Canon Law, which was looked upon as part of unnecessary Catholic "ideology" invented to protect the interests of the church hierarchy. Instead, religious legislation was integrated in general political legislation and was issued by the political authorities. The early modern Anabaptists offer an exception here: for a long time they remained outside secular legislation, asserting the fundamental gap between secular legislation and the rules of their religious community.

Protestantism and Protestantisation

In sum: Through the four centuries since the Reformation, some fundamental Protestant ideals have contributed deeply to transforming and differentiating the Christian religion. Varieties of Protestant Christianity have demonstrated a remarkable ability to adapt to new circumstances, without departing from some key characteristics of being Protestant.

The point of departure for this volume is not the Weberian thesis, even if it is still a fascinating contribution to research on Protestantism. Neither does the volume intend to contribute to a normative (theological) discussion on Protestantism as such, nor to elaborate further on historical varieties of Protestant religion. Instead, the aim of the volume is to look closer into the question of how Protestantism is not just a specific confessional part of Christianity, but also a pattern or model for religious change and religious transformation in Modernity.

A few researchers have previously asked similar questions and proposed some answers.[4] Two prominent sociologists of religion will be particularly mentioned here: both of them have used the concept "Protestantisation" to characterise this specific kind of transforming or formatting religion according to Protestant patterns.

Peter Berger

The first is Peter Berger in his short paper "Pluralism, Protestantisation, and the Voluntary Principle" (Berger, 2007). Berger discusses several types of Protestantism, but his argument is based on the concepts *voluntarism* and *individualism* as the key characteristics of the Protestant tradition.

> Catholic observers have coined the term Protestantization to refer, usually pejoratively, to recent changes in their church. Stripped of its pejorative undertone, it is rather an apt term. Sometimes it describes doctrinal change…But the term is most apt in describing social changes within the church – to wit, the role of an increasingly assertive laity, the transformation of the church into a de facto denomination, and one doctrinal change that is definitely relevant here – the theological undergirding of the norm of religious liberty (p. 25).

According to this definition of the core of Protestantism, its ultimate expressions are to be found within Protestant denominations, particularly within the Pentecostal movement – which is also the most successful variety of Protestantism in a global perspective: "The amazing cross-national success of Pentecostalism and other forms of popular Protestantism can in no small measure be explained by a distinctive capacity to operate as voluntary associations."

The context of Peter Berger's argument is a discussion of religion and democracy. Here, a Protestantisation of religious traditions (including certain tendencies in the Catholic Church) is mainly regarded as a positive development, since Protestant types of religion, according to Berger's concept of Protestantisation, are usually easily adaptable to pluralist societies.

---

4   For an overview of recent approaches to these questions from various research fields, see Aarsheim (2018).

Oliver Roy

More recently, the French political scientist Oliver Roy made use of the Protestantisation concept within a quite different context. In his book *Holy Ignorance: When Religion and Culture Part Ways* (Roy, 2013), he discusses Protestantisation as part of a more general contemporary change taking place within the field of religion. According to Roy, today we can observe a process of standardization of religion, where religion is being *formatted* according to general patterns. This formatting of religion can take place both top-down and bottom-up, and Protestant ideals play an essential role in these processes.

An example of the top-down Protestantisation of religion is related to the legal sphere: Roy describes a ruling from Florida in 1997, whereby "The court imposed a Protestant vision of religion on Catholics and Jews, the consequence of which is explicitly to distinguish cultural markers, considered as non-essential, from religious markers." Theology belonged to religion's "high tradition" and was more essential than the different parts of a "little tradition" which includes religiosity, folklore, customs, beliefs (the culture).[5]

Another example also comes from the US. When in in the nineteenth century Catholic bishops in the US insisted on a separation between church and state, and opposed a boiled-down Christianity in the form of "civil religion", they were trying to avoid being Protestantised.[6]

Protestantism and Secularity

Structurally, Protestant formatting of religion most often takes place as a process of reduction and concentration. Characteristic institutional and ritual attributes of traditional religion become less important, and in many cases become totally irrelevant. This dynamic of reduction has encouraged several debates about the relationship between Protestantism and Secularization: Is Protestant formatting of religion a preparation for or a strategy of secularization? And how are Protestant and secular ideals related to each other?

A new debate on these questions was raised in Brad Gregory's *The Unintended Reformation: How a Religious Revolution Secularized Society* (Gregory, 2012). To Gregory, the unintended effects of the Reformation include "an absence of shared answers to Life Questions" and "a hyperpluralism of divergent secular and religious truth claims" (Gregory, 2012: 377). Truth claims during the Reformation

---

5 Roy (2013), 204.
6 Roy (2013), 199.

were legitimized by an appeal to Scripture alone. But the Protestant *sola scriptura* principle did not, according to Gregory, "yield the desired result". The Protestants "disagreed about the meaning and the prioritization of biblical texts, and the relationship of those texts to doctrines regarding the sacraments, worship, grace, the church and so forth" (Gregory, 2012, 109). In this way Protestant strategies become self-destructive, and their truth claims are gradually replaced by secularized and specialized knowledge.

Gregory is a historian, teaching at a Catholic university. His story about the unintended effects of the Reformation is a quite sad tale, without a happy ending. However, recent research on Protestantism also offers other views on the relationship between Protestant formatting of religion and modern Secularity. From a Lutheran theological point of view, the secular world may at the same time be seen as a world created by God, and therefore not different from or opposite to another specific "religious" sphere of rituals, churches and pastors. In this way, Protestant "religion" is extended in order to also affirm and include secularity.

This line of argument has primarily been presented in a Nordic context, where so-called "creation theology" has for decades played an important role in theological research. A recent contribution with a very different approach to the relationship between Protestantism and secularity is the volume *Reformation Theology for a Post Secular Age: Løgstrup, Prenter, Wingren and the Future of Scandinavian Creation Theology* (Gregersen, Uggla & Wyller, 2017).

The chapters

Most of the chapters in the present volume were presented in draft versions at a conference in Oslo in 2017. Two deal with ways of formatting religion in accordance with a Protestant pattern. Oddbjørn Leirvik takes Oliver Roy as his point of departure for discussing developments within contemporary Islam, whereas Gina Lende presents an elaborate analysis of a specific and highly relevant variety of contemporary formatting of Protestant religion: the "Pentecostalization" taking place in recent years in many parts of the world.

Karin Neutel and Vebjørn Horsfjord present a specific case: contemporary discussions on circumcision. Drawing on sources from Norway and Germany, Karin Neutel discusses challenges of identifying "religion" in a context of legislation and jurisdiction, and problems arising from a "Protestant" preconception of "religion" in actual court cases related to circumcision. Vebjørn Horsfjord offers an in-depth discussion of texts from two central contributors to the Norwegian debate on circumcision, and demonstrates how the argument in these texts is implicitly and unconsciously dominated by Protestant or Protestant-secular preconceptions.

Three of the articles deal mainly with the relationship between Protestantism and secularity. On the one hand, Erlend From analyses the protestant context of Norwegian "Non-religion". Here, Protestantism is a point of departure for leaving the whole thing called religion behind as a matter neither worth defending nor fighting. On the other hand, in their chapters Trygve Wyller and Allen Jorgenson elaborate on different aspects of modern secularity, discussing it not as an "unintended" consequence of the Lutheran reformation, but rather as an inherent dimension of Lutheran theology.

Literature

Berger, Peter (2007). "Pluralism, Protestantization, and the Voluntary Principle", In Thomas Banchoff (ed.): *Democracy and the New Religious Pluralism*, Oxford 2007, 20–29.

Ehrenpreis, Stefan and Ute Lotz-Heumann (2002). *Reformation und konfessionelles Zeitalter* (Series: "Kontroversen um die Geschichte"), Darmstadt: Wissenschaftliche Buchgesellschaft.

Gregersen, Niels Henrik; Bengt Kristensson Uggla and Trygve Wyller (eds.) (2017). *Reformation theology for a Post Secular Age: Løgstrup, Prenter, Wingren and the Future of Scandinavian Creation Theology* (= Studies in Contemporary Religion, vol. 24), Göttingen: Vandenhoeck & Ruprecht.

Hamm, Berndt (1992). *Reformation* als *normative Zentrierung von Religion und Gesell - schaft*, In: Jahrbuch für Biblische Theologie 7 (1992), 241 – 279.

Käsler, Dirk (2014). *Max Weber. Eine Biographie*, Munich: H.C.Beck 2014.

Reinhard, Wolfgang and Heinz Schilling (ed.) (1995): *Die katholische Konfessionalisierung* (= "Schriften des Vereins für Reformationsgeschichte", vol. 198), Heidelberg: Verein für Reformationsgeschichte/Gütersloher Verlagshaus.

Roy, Oliver (2013). *Holy Ignorance: When Religion and Culture part ways.*

von Scheliha, Arnulf and Markus Schröder (eds.) (1998). *Das protestantische Prinzip. Historische und systematische Studien zum Protestantismusbegriff*, Stuttgart: W. Kohlhammer.

Aarsheim, Helge (2018). *Protestantisering og Protestantisme: Kilden til demokratisering, økonomisk utvikling og rettslig orden?* In: Kirke og Kultur 123 (2018), 16–23 (DOI DOI: 10.18261/issn.1504–3002-2018-01-03).

Oddbjørn Leirvik

Chapter 2: Protestantisation of Islam – as Good, Humanistic Religion

Introductory observations

In literature that applies the term "Protestantism" in connection with Islam, two quite contradictory features may be identified. In popular as well as scholarly writings, Islamic Protestantism (or Protestant Islam) seems mainly to connote "good religion". It tends to be associated with liberal values, such as individualism, lay religion, intellectual freedom, political liberalism, and even humanism. But there is also a wide array of opposite examples where Protestant Islam is perceived as bad, fundamentalist religion.

In this chapter, polemic examples of how Protestant Islam is perceived as something bad (even dangerous) will first be identified, and then emic references to good, Protestant Islam will be cited and discussed – with particular references to the Turkish and Iranian contexts.

In the second part, and in a more etic approach, a possible nexus between "Protestant" and "humanistic" Islam will be considered. Here, the contextual references will be Norway and Germany, and the (Protestant) legacy of "university theology" as it has been developed on northern European soil. The analysis will be informed by Olivier Roy's "formatting of religion" and Edvard Said's "traveling theory".

Several attempts have been made, through historical analysis, to identify structural similarities between the European Reformations in the sixteenth and seventeenth centuries and modern reform movements in Islam, for instance in Sub-Saharan Africa, or in Middle Eastern Islamism (Loimeier, 2017; Utvik, 1997). While this is an interesting line of research in itself, there is not enough space here to allow a critical engagement with historical issues. I will restrict myself to an analysis of contemporary discourses on "good" and "bad" Protestantism in Islam, and the emergence of a discourse of "Islamic humanism" which seems to draw upon notions of good Protestantism.

The following discussion also does not analyze the pervasive talk of a "reformation" or "reform" of Islam, epitomized by Abdullahi Ahmed An-Na'im's book title from 1990: . It goes without saying, however, that the discourse of a Protestant Islam (perceived as "good religion") draws upon and reflects the much larger discussion of a (desirable) Islamic reformation.

Protestant formatting and traveling ideas

In my critical (etic) analysis of the mentioned discursive examples, I will use Roy's notion of formatting religion, which includes the perspective of "self-formatting". Particular attention with be paid to the notion of humanism in these discursive developments.

Olivier Roy's book *Holy Ignorance* (2013) associates "Protestantisation" with the kind of standardization of religion that takes place "when religion and culture part ways" (which is also the subtitle of his book). Roy sees Protestantism thus as strongly associated with de-culturalization. The eagerness to separate religion from culture reflects a will to reform which may (in Roy's perception) either express itself as confrontational particularism (neofundamentalism) or as dialogical universalism (humanist, ethical Islam).

Roy's use of the term Protestantisation is not very pointed but seems to designate a dominant pattern in an ongoing standardization of religion (Roy, 2013: 187ff). The Protestant format of religion, which in Roy's opinion has become thoroughly globalized, is characterized by phenomena such as privatization of religious practice, de-ethnicization, churchification (a joint pattern for how religions functions are institutionalized (Roy, 2013: 190)), and formalized notions of religion that suit the need for legal regulation (Roy, 2013: 195–200).

According to Roy, Protestantisation in an Islamic context does not necessarily challenge established dogmas but shifts the emphasis from faith to morals:

> Formatting has not always operated in favour of fundamentalism, as we have seen for liberal Jews in the United States, and it is probable that the West today is witnessing the emergence of an Islam that is 'liberal' in its practice if not in its theological thinking (Roy, 2013: 208, cf. 196.).

If we combine Roy's notion of Protestant Islam in *Holy Ignorance* with his depiction of ethical, humanistic Islam in *Globalised Islam*, we may also expect that Protestantisation shifts the emphasis from casuistic law to a democratized form of ethical reflection based on general values rather than unchangeable norms:

> Norms are reformulated in terms of values, and are subsequently 'negotiable', meaning that the issue is not to follow the letter but the spirit of the law (Roy, 2004: 190).

For Roy, Protestantisation is a dominant mode of formatting religion in the globalized age. Protestant formatting may either be induced from above (top-down) or express itself as "self-formatting" (bottom-up, cf. Roy, 2004: 196). In the latter form, formatting of religion may also be seen as a "dialogical" process:

By dialogical, we mean a process where the combination of confrontation and dialogue ends up by creating a new, relatively consensual equilibrium, because the actors, far from defending closed, preconceived systems, reformulate their own position in the debate with the other (Roy, 2013: 191).

Roy gives as an example of consensual adaptation "the redefinition of *sharia* as a system of voluntary norms" which

... allows Muslims to think of themselves as still being within the framework of Qur'anic law and 'secular' Muslims to consider that unacceptable punishments (the *hudud*) have been consigned to oblivion (Roy, 2013: 191).

Roy's perception of formatting processes may leave the impression of determining, sociological processes or even top-down political measures. Roy's understanding of formatting is toned down, however, by his notion of "self-formatting", which allows for a larger space for bottom-up, reformist agency.

Self-formatting processes in Roy's sense can also be seen in a different light, namely as the continuous application of ideas which may "travel" from one generation or context to another. In his analysis of the discourse of Protestant Islam in Iran, Sukidi leans on Edward W. Said's notion of "traveling theory":

Like peoples and schools of criticism, ideas and theories travel – from person to person, from situation to situation, and from one period to another. Cultural and intellectual life are usually nourished and often sustained by this circulation of ideas, and whether it takes the form of acknowledged or unconscious influence, creative borrowing, or wholesome appropriation, the movement of ideas and theories from one place to another is both a fact of life and a usefully enabling condition of intellectual activity (Said, 1983: 226).

So what are we dealing with here when trying to understand what "Protestant Islam" may mean? Formatting of religion, in accordance with global trends that can be analyzed with the tools of sociology of religion? Or are we witness to a free borrowing of notions, remolded to suit contextual needs? I will suggest that the perspectives of "self-formatting" and "traveling theory" complement each other, when trying to understand processes and discourses related to a possible "Protestantisation" of Islam.

Bad Protestantism

The discourse of Protestant Islam does not, as Roy demonstrates, necessarily signify good religion. From an etic perspective, Islamic Protestantism may also, as in Olivier Roy's books *Globalized Islam* (2004) and *Holy Ignorance* (2013), be associated with a more problematic form of Protestantism which Roy calls "neofundamentalism" (Roy, 2004: 232ff).

As an emic parallel, and in a cautionary mode, Mohammed al-Abbasi speaks of radical Salafis as "Protestant Muslims", characterized by their aggressive puritanism and their divisive effect on the Muslim community.[1] The association of Salafi (or Wahhabi) puritan radicalism with Protestant religion seems in fact to be quite widespread on the internet, in sweeping generalizations like the following quote from Shahab Shabbir:

> [Q:] What is the similarity between the Wahabi movement in Islam and the Protestant movement in Christianity?
> [A:] Both movements appear to be promoting puritanism in their respective religious set up, still they have proven disastrous to the rich heritage of the world's two major faiths (Shabbir, 2012).

A similar link between Salafism and Protestantism is made by Alexander Thurston in an article on Salafism in Nigeria, in which the author suggests "that Salafism may be closer to Protestantism than to Catholicism". In Thurston's view, "there are interesting comparisons to be made between Salafism and Protestantism in terms of how each tradition constructs authority". As "[N]either Salafism, nor Sunni Islam generally, has a centralized authority" […] "Salafis and their intellectual forebears are the closest Muslim equivalents to Martin Luther in recent centuries" (Thurston, 2017).

In Thurston's article, Islam might seem to have become a proxy for intra-Christian strides between Catholicism and Protestantism. In a cruder and cautionary manner, Francis Lynch of the conservative Catholic "Faith Movement" sees fundamental similarities between Protestantism and Islam in such issues as scriptural fundamentalism, anti-sacramentalism, radical individualism and (dissolvable) marriages. In conclusion, Lynch suggests "that many of the major Protestant innovations have a relationship with Islam" (Lynch, 2007).

---

[1] "Predictably enough, our own Islamic Protestantism, like that of Calvin, Luther and Cromwell, has in practice yielded division rather than unity, and mental and cultural poverty rather than a new brilliance. Not only are the Muslim Protestants (Salafis, as they inaccurately call themselves) at loggerheads with traditional orthodox ulema, but they find it notoriously hard to agree among themselves" (Al-Abbasi, n.d.).

In the cited examples of popular comparisons between Islam and Protestant Islam, (salafi or mainstream) Islam clearly stands out as "bad" religion. It may also, however, be associated with "good", liberal and humanistic, religion. Although Roy's primary research interest lies in Protestant neofundamentalism (including Salafism), he also recognizes an "ethical" version of Protestant Islam which he (albeit in passing) associates with "humanism" (Roy, 2004: 187ff).[2] In emic as well as etic discourses, Protestant Islam may thus signify either (bad) neofundamentalism or (good) humanistic religion.

From a different perspective, Protestantism (as good religion) may also be contrasted against Islam (as bad religion). When in 1990 the Norwegian artist Rolv Wesenlund (addressing a church audience) warned against the growth of Islam in Norway, he called for mobilization of "our Norwegian, Protestant belief" against Islam "which is not a tolerant faith" (Leirvik, 2016a: 58).

In such brief references to Protestantism it is not always clear what is meant by this loaded term. In other cases, however, the cue of Protestantism comes with a more explicit content. In what follows, (emic) examples will be taken from Muslim reformist discourses in Iran and Turkey in which Protestant Islam connotes liberal and/or humanistic religion. I will also note a similar discursive development in the works of Mouhanad Khorchide, a representative of the new centers for Islamic theology at German universities, and in a group of reformist Muslims in Norway.

Good Protestants in Iran and Turkey

Moving on from Roy's reflections on globalized Protestantism (be it humanistic or neo-fundamentalist) I will offer two examples of how the term Islamic Protestantism has been used in the Iranian and Turkish contexts respectively (in both cases, with emic reference to "good" religion).

In the Iranian context, in 2002 the reformist thinker Hashem Aghajari published a famous speech titled "A Call for Islamic Protestantism" (Aghajari, 2002). The speech earned him a death sentence which was, however, reduced to five years' imprisonment. Reflecting the theocratic context of Iran, Aghajari is particularly interested in the anti-clerical aspect of Protestantism.[3] In a positive vein, he associates Islamic Protestantism with lay religion and religious democratization – focused on the right to "to understand the Koran on your own" (Aghajari, 2002).

---

2 "Humanism, ethical Islam and Salvation".
3 The anti-clerical aspect of Protestantism has also been applied analytically with reference to the famous reformist Abdolkarim Soroush's criticism of the Shi'ite clergy (see Amirpur, 1996).

In an interesting analysis, leaning on Edward Said, the Indonesian scholar Sukidi mentions Aghajari as an example of how "the traveling idea of Islamic Protestantism" has been appropriated by what he calls the "Iranian Luthers". Sukidi notes the successive admiration of Luther by the Iranian reformist thinkers al-Afghani (d. 1897),[4] Shari'ati (d. 1977),[5] and Aghajari. In a documented chain of inspiration, these thinkers (as Sukidi reads them) made anti-authoritarian, Islamic Protestantism a "traveling idea" in the Iranian context.[6]

As for Aghajari, he seems to associate Islamic Protestantism with Roy's humanistic form of de-culturalized religion. Actually, he identifies his call for Islamic Protestantism with a call for Islamic humanism: "Today's Islam [should be] 'core Islam,' not 'traditional Islam.' Islamic Protestantism is logical, practical and humanist. It is thoughtful and progressive" (Aghajari, 2002). As for humanist values, promoted by Islamic Protestantism, Aghajari includes the rights of religious minorities, denunciation of cruel punishments, and gender equality.

In the Turkish context, Hakan Yavus has offered an interesting analysis of the modernizing Gülen movement (vilified by the government after being accused of the attempted coup in 2016) as a form of Protestantism. In the context of steady economic growth in Turkey, Yavus associates Islamic Protestantism with pious capitalism and political liberalism. Referring to Weber and "the intrinsic connection between an ascetic lifestyle and a capitalist form of economic activity," Yavus notes that the Gülen movement "promotes innerworldly asceticism, rationalization of daily life, and hard work and austere life style." In Yavus' affirmative reference to the Gülen movement's Protestant values, numerous references to the good of humanity and humanizing processes can be found. Describing the movement's perceived good, Yavus clearly sees it as a humanizing force: "The movement has been seeking to transform the world by humanizing socioeconomic conditions for the glory of God" (Yavus, 2013: 118f).

---

4 "Al-Afghani strongly argued that Islam needed a Luther in order to achieve a Protestant-type of Islamic reform. In brief, the basic foundation of a Protestant-type of Islamic reform included the principles that: (1) similar to Luther's call for a return to the Bible, al-Afghani's Islamic reform was a return to the Qur'an alone as the progressive scripture; and (2) the door of rational interpretation of the Qur'an (ijtihad) should be reopened in order to reinvent the true spirit of the Qur'an in accord with reason, progress, and civilization." (Sukidi, 2005: 404f.)

5 "Believing that Islam and its Iranian clerical establishment required a fundamental reform, Shari'ati insisted on the need for the model provided by Luther and Calvin for transferring the establishment of the Iranian clerical institution to the leadership of progressive intelligentsia ..." (Sukidi, 2005: 406).

6 "The idea of Islamic Protestantism traveled from al-Afghani to Ali Shari'ati. A number of his public lectures and writings seemed to support the idea that he followed al-Afghani's call for a Protestant-type of Islamic reform [...] he openly praised al-Afghani as the progressive intellectual who had raised up and spread Islamic Protestantism" (Sukidi, 2005: 410).

In sum, both the Iranian and the Turkish examples could be seen as instances of "self-formatting" in Roy's sense. The references to "Islamic Protestantism" and "Iranian Luthers" can also be analyzed as traveling ideas that become meaningful in particular contexts. Aghajari calls for Islamic Protestantism in his resistance to authoritarian theocracy, in search for what he calls a humanistic Islam. In Yavus' sympathetic analysis of the quasi-Protestant Gülen movement, political liberalization and humanization of the economy are seen as desired outcomes of the movement's pious form of capitalism – by what might seem to be an emic application of well-known Weberian theories.[7]

Islamic university theology in Europe: fostering protestant, humanistic Islam?

The cited (emic) examples of how liberal, Islamic reform is being associated with Protestantism may be taken as a tendency to inscribe reformist ideas in larger, universalistic discourses. As noted, this includes the discourse of humanism which is regularly alluded to when reformist Islam is associated with liberal forms of Protestantism – as can be seen in Roy, Aghajari and Yavus.

The cases to be dealt with in the following represent a discourse that is not centered around the notion of Protestantism, but rather its (as it might seem) conceptual neighbor of humanism. The cases are taken from the northern European context and humanist discourses among Muslim reform thinkers.

In recent decades new centers and study programs in Islamic theology have been established within the framework of secular universities in northern Europe. In Germany, from 2010 onwards, five new centers for Islamic theology have been established as separate units at state universities. In the Netherlands and Scandinavia, in the same period, chairs and study programs in Islamic theology have been introduced by the existing Protestant faculties of theology.

Some of these initiatives have been dubbed "Islamic university theology" (Leirvik, 2016b). Historically, this term has been associated with Protestant theology as done in a secular university, and infused with the liberal values conventionally associated with Protestantism (alternatively, humanism).

According to David Tracy, Christian theology has three "publics": the church, the academy and the wider society.[8] As for greater society as an intended public of university theology, Perry Schmidt-Leukel of the University of Münster relates his

---

7 Sukidi (2006) analyzes the ideology of the Indonesian reform movement Muhammadiya as an instance of Protestant ethic – against Weber's own perception that Islam is the polar opposite of the Protestant ethic. For an earlier discussion of Islam, capitalism and "the Weber Theses", see Turner, 1974.
8 Tracy, 1991: 3, 5.

understanding of the European legacy of doing theology in secular environments to the very idea of *universitas* (which is, of course, much older than the modern notion of secularity). He argues that only when confessional theology refers itself to questions of universal truth and relates its work to the totality of reality – that is, to *universitas* – can it defend its place in the university (Schmidt-Leukel, 2013: 33). This means that, in his view, the university has no place for a theology that is merely cultivation of tradition for the faith communities to consume.

Corresponding visions of public theology, oriented towards the *universitas*, are being articulated from the new chairs and centers for Islamic theology in western European universities. In the first issue of a new journal of Islamic-theological studies, published by the center in Frankfurt, Bekim Agai and colleagues use the term "Universitätstheologie" to describe a tripartite public consisting of the Islamic faith communities, society at large, and the academy (Agai, 2015). Ömer Özsoy, from the same center, speaks of a self-reflexive Islamic theology which – when done in a university context and in a post-metaphysic way (Habermas) – may become an inspiration for society in its entirety (Özsoy, 2015: 62).

For the first time in history, Özsoy says, Muslim intellectuals are now able to express themselves in the first person in the European university context marked by modern philosophy and post-Enlightenment scientific tradition. In a self-formatting mode, Öszoy goes on: "This encounter will probably not only change the perception of Islam in a fundamental way but also take the scientific endeavor of Islamic theology a considerable step forward" (Özsoy, 2015: 66).[9]

It is too early to say what kind of formatting of Islamic theology that will take place in this new framework, although some tendencies can be discerned. As noted by the Danish researcher Birgitte Schepelern Johansen, who has been researching some of these initiatives, "…several institutions providing education on Islamic theology, private as well as public, have chosen a strategy of what could be called 'universal Islam'" (Johansen, 2008: 455).

It might thus be expected that the location within a university context shifts the emphasis of Islamic theology from tradition-specific disciplines to more general subjects – for instance, from Islamic jurisprudence to ethics (cf. Roy's ethical Islam); from doctrine to the philosophy of religion; and (in general) from religion-specific traditionalism to de-culturalized universalism.

Many of the new centers and chairs referred to above have been initiated by the political authorities, as a formatting from above. I would nevertheless argue that the initiatives also reflect a self-formatting ambition in parts of the Muslim community to develop the theological and philosophical legacy of Islam in a secular state university context.

---

9 Translated from German by the author.

Researching these tendencies, a power-critical perspective is certainly necessary. In view of the fact that many of the cited developments have been facilitated by fresh money from the political authorities, Schepelern Johansen suggests that

> [p]ublic institutionalized and formalized education becomes a way of influencing Muslim religious authorities and thereby Muslims in general. European politicians seem to want to reshape Islamic discourses, practices and organizational forms similar to those devised for Christianity…(Johansen, 2008: 450).

Perhaps Islamic university theology – financed by fresh money from the governments or the universities – represents a formatting from above, as a political promotion of good Islamic religion. In my view, however, the new centers, chairs, and programs of Islamic theology also reflect a conscious self-formatting on the part of Muslim intellectuals who are searching for new platforms for doing reformist theology – in the legacy of Protestant university theology.

Humanistic Islam

As noted, those who – in a positive vein – associate Islamic reform with Protestantism also tend to link Protestantism with humanism, a term that is often explicated further but seems nevertheless to function as a most important marker in Islamic reformist discourses (Leirvik, 2020). In what follows, I will highlight two recent books about humanism written by northern European Muslims. I am referring first to an anthology titled "Islamic humanism" (*Islamsk humanisme*, from 2016) written by a group of reform-oriented Norwegian Muslims – many of them with a university affiliation, and second to the book entitled "God believes in the human being. With Islam towards a new humanism" (*Gott glaubt an den Menschen: Mit dem Islam zu einem neuen Humanismus*, from 2015), written by the director of the Centre for Islamic Theology at the University of Münster, Mouhanad Khorchide.

In the book on Islamic humanism published by Norwegian Muslims, the human rights activist and convert to Islam Lena Larsen criticizes Muslim attempts to circumscribe human rights conventions by referring to Sharia-based regulations which provide legitimacy to anti-humanist practices, such as "discrimination of women and minorities, brutal forms of punishment and limited freedom of expression" (Larsen in Noor and Reiss, 2016: 41).[10] It is also interesting to note how in this book, ethical normativity is anchored in lived experiences and modern sensibilities more than in Sharia: "Objections and critique cannot be repudiated by the argument that

---

10 Translation from Norwegian by the author.

Sharia-based regulations are not subject to change. Modern human beings regard slavery and gender discrimination as unjust, they regard freedom of religion to be an innate right, and hold that cruel and denigrating punishment shall not be tolerated" (Larsen, 2016: 47).[11]

In general, the book propounds "an Islam in harmony with the fundamental values in modern humanism, such as the human being's self-determination and innate dignity, democratic activity, human rights, socio-political justice and an optimistic view of rationality and reason" (Shah, 2016: 133).[12]

Although Protestantism is not mentioned as a frame of reference in this particular book, the perceived humanist values come close to those conventionally associated with Protestantism in its "good" modality. It also strikes me that in this kind of reasoning, humanistic values function as non-negotiables, trumping important aspects of the ethical or juristic tradition of Islam. But the book's critique is primarily aimed at traditional perceptions and practices (again, a Protestant form of discourse). The normative sources (especially the Qur'an) tend to be taken in the very best sense, sometimes implying that true Islam is inherently humanistic.

The other book, written by Mouhanad Khorchide, invokes the European humanist tradition in a project explicitly aimed at humanizing Islamic theology. The book is written from within the context of the secular European university and indicates how Islamic university theology in the European context is currently being reformulated in dialogue with dominant ethical and philosophical discourses in the greater society. Khorchides's main focus is on the humanistic legacy in its confrontation with inhumane traditions.

The most central issue in this book is religion and violence, a theme that Khorchide (on behalf of the Muslim community) approaches in a highly self-critical way. He criticizes the apologetic argument that "violence has nothing to do with Islam" and cites a number of mainstream classical scholars in Islamic history who have actually articulated rather belligerent interpretations of the Qur'an (Khorchide, 2015: 179ff).

Khorchide does not stop at ethics (cf. Roy's perception of Islamic Protestantism as purely ethical) but criticizes theological conceptions as well. As in one of his previous works on divine mercy (*Islam ist Barmherzigkeit*, 2012), Khorchide sharply criticizes violent images of perdition and of hell as a place of divine torture, calling instead for a humanistic pedagogy of religion.

In another of Khorchide's books, *Scharia – der missverstandene Gott* (2013), which carries the programmatic subtitle "Der Weg zu einer modernen islamischen Ethik", he makes it clear from the outset that he (as a good Protestant?) will not focus

---

11 Translation from Norwegian by the author.
12 Translation from Norwegian by the author.

on the juristic aspects of Sharia but rather on its "ethical" and "spiritual" aspects (Khorchide, 2013: 74f., 95). He also mentions that when a new professorship in Islamic law was about to be announced in Münster, they changed the title from Islamic law to "Normenlehre und deren Methodologie" ("Science of norms and its methodology"), again to avoid a juristic understanding of Sharia and with the positive aim of contributing to a general discussion on ethical norms in pluralistic societies (Khorchide, 2013: 85).

In his positive formulation of a liberating pedagogy and a non-violent humanism, Khorchide leans both on his reading of Islam as a religion of mercy and on relevant strands of European humanism, which are expounded at length. Islamic-religious and European-philosophical tradition seem thus to carry equal weight as background material for his reflections on Islam's contribution to humanism today. For instance, he explains how the Islamic tradition of God's qualities can be transposed to human ideals.

Conclusion

It is debatable whether Islamic, humanist discourses anchored in the European university context can be linked with discourses of Protestantism in other contexts. At the conceptual level, Khorchide does not call for a Protestant reformation of Islam. His key notion is humanism. From a meta-perspective, however, it seems that the concrete values associated with ("good") Protestantism and humanism respectively seem to be almost interchangeable. In the background of this discursive construction lurk "bad", fundamentalist forms of Protestantism, against which humanist Protestantism and university theology (according to its proponents) need to get mobilized.

In these ways, Islamic Protestantism (and humanism) may have become both a widespread way of self-formatting and a "traveling idea" in Edward Said's sense – journeying through "phases of acceptance, modification, and a new reinterpretation" (Sukidi, 2005: 411)[13] capable of forming new clusters of meaning in shifting contexts; and with a strong affinity between perceived "Protestant" and "humanist" values.

---

13 Citing Said, 1983: 226.

Bibliography

Agai, Bekim et al. (2014). "Islamische Theologie in Deutschland. Herausforderungen im Spanningsfeld divergierender Erwartungen." *Frankfurter Zeitschrift für Islamisch-Theologishe Studien* 1, 7–28.

Al-Abbasi, Mohammed. "Protestant Islam" (n.d.) (http://www.masud.co.uk/ISLAM/misc/pislam.htm).

Aghajari, Hashem (2002). "From monkey to man. A call for Islamic Protestantism". *The Iranian*, December 4. (https://iranian.com/Opinion/2002/December/Aghajari/?site=archive) [last accessed 6 Jan. 2021]

Amirpur, Katajun (1996). "An Iranian Luther? 'Abdolkarîm Sorûsh's criticism of the Shiite clergy." *Orient* 3, 465–482.

An-Na'im, Abdullahi Ahmed (1990). *Toward an Islamic Reformation. Civil Liberties, Human Rights, and International Law*. Syracuse: Syracuse University Press.

Johansen, Birgitte Schepelern (2008). "Legitimizing Islamic Theology at European Universities." In Willem B. Drees and Peter Sjoerd van Koningsveld (eds.): *The Study of Religion and the Training of Muslim Clergy in Europe. Academic and Religious Freedom in the 21st Century*. Leiden: Leiden University Press.

Khorchide, Mouhanad (2015). *Gott glaubt an den Menschen: Mit dem Islam zu einem neuen Humanismus*. Freiburg im Breisgau: Herder.

Khorchide, Mouhanad (2013). *Scharia – der missverstandene Gott*. Freiburg im Breisgau: Herder.

Khorchide, Mouhanad (2012). *Islam ist Barmherzigkeit*. Freiburg im Breisgau: Herder.

Larsen, Lena. (2016). "Islam og menneskerettigheter". In Noor, Linda and Ellen Reiss (eds.). *Islamsk humanisme*. Oslo: Moment, 64–87.

Leirvik, Oddbjørn (2020). "Islamic humanism or humanistic Islam?" *Interreligious Studies and Intercultural Theology* 4, no. 1, 88–101.

Leirvik, Oddbjørn (2016b). "Islamic University Theology". *Studia Theologica* 70, no. 2, 127–144.

Leirvik, Oddbjørn (2016). *Religionspluralisme. Mangfald, konflikt og dialog i Norge*. Oslo: Pax.

Loimeier, Roman (2005). "Is There Something like 'Protestant Islam'?" *Die Welt des Islam* 45, no. 2, 216–254.

Lynch, Francis (2007). "Islam, Protestantism and Divergence from Catholicism." *FAITH-Magazine*, January-February.

Noor, Linda and Ellen Reiss (eds.) (2016). *Islamsk humanisme*. Oslo: Moment.

Roy, Olivier (2004). *Globalized Islam. The Search for a New Ummah*. New York: Columbia University Press.

Roy, Olivier (2013). *Holy Ignorance. When Religion and Culture Part Ways*. Oxford: Oxford University Press.

Said, Edward W. (1983). *The World, the Text, and the Critic.* Cambridge, MA: Harvard University Press.

Schmidt-Leukel, Perry (2013). "Interreligiöse Theologie und die Theologie der Zukunft." In Bernhardt, Reinhold and Perry Schmidt-Leukel (Hrsg., 2013) *Interreligiöse Theologie. Chancen und Probleme.* Zürich: Theologischer Verlag Zürich.

Shabbir, Shahab (2012). "What is the similarity between the Wahabi movement in Islam and the Protestant movement in Christianity." Researchgate 10 October. (https://www.researchgate.net/post/What_is_the_similarity_between_the_Wahabi_movement_in_Islam_and_the_Protestant_movement_in_Christianity) [last accessed 6 Jan. 2021]

Shah, Farhan (2016). "Islamsk humanism". In Noor, Linda and Ellen Reiss (eds.). *Islamsk humanisme.* Oslo: Moment, 24–30.

Sukidi (2005). "The traveling idea of Islamic Protestantism: A study of Iranian Luthers." *Islam and Christian-Muslim Relations* 16, no. 4, October, 401–412.

Sukidi (2006). "Max Weber's remarks on Islam: The Protestant Ethic among Muslim puritans." *Islam and Christian-Muslim Relations* 17, no. 2, April, 195–205.

Thurston, Alexander (2017). "Salafism in Nigeria. An Introduction." *The Immanent Frame,* 11 April (https://tif.ssrc.org/2017/04/11/salafism-in-nigeria/) [last accessed 6 Jan. 2021]

Tracy, David (1991). *The Analogical Imagination. Christian Theology and the Culture of Pluralism.* New York: Crossroad.

Turner, Bryan S. (1974). "Islam, Capitalism and the Weber Theses." *The British Journal of Sociology* 25, no. 2, 230–243.

Utvik, Bjørn Olav (1997). "Islamism – Cromwell's Ghost in the Middle East." In Stein Tønnesen, Juhani Koponen, Niels Steensgard and Thommy Svensson (eds.). *Between National Histories and Global History.* Helsinki: Suomen Historiallinen Seura, 129–42.

Yavus, Hakan (2013). *Toward an Islamic Enlightenment: The Gülen Movement.* Oxford: OUP.

Özsoy, Ömer (2015). "Islamische Theologie als Wissenschaft. Funktionen, Methoden, Argumentationen." In Gharaibeh, Mohammed, Esnaf Begic, Hansjörg Schmid and Christian Ströbele (eds.) *Zwischen Glaube und Wissenschaft: Theologie in Christentum und Islam.* Regensburg: Pustet, 56–68.

Gina Lende

Chapter 3: The Protestant Newcomer

Politics, Economics and Pentecostal Growth

Introduction

The explosive growth of Pentecostalism since, in particular, the 1970s, has altered the religious landscape in the world. In Africa and Latin America, this change has been particularly spectacular. In Latin America the close to monopolist role of the Catholic Church has been broken, and in Africa the popularity of the newcomers has significantly challenged and changed the way the older mainline churches do religion. Research has focused on the defining characteristics of an increasingly diverse Pentecostal movement, and on how the growth in this movement has affected mainline Churches and other religions. Equally important is the interest in how this development affects society, outside the explicit Pentecostal domain.

As a Protestant newcomer, the Pentecostal movement rarely figures in the more focused protestantisation-literature. Yet, many of the same questions raised with Protestantism, such as a possible correlation between democracy and modernity, as well as a proposed affinity with economic growth, are very much present in the research on Pentecostalism. As explicit examples, we have the influential sociologist Peter L. Berger who in 2010 wrote the article entitled "Max Weber is alive and well, living in Guatemala: The Protestant ethic of today". In a similar manner, working on the African continent, Dena Freeman titled her much cited work on religion and development "The Pentecostal Ethic and the Spirit of Development" (2016). Nonetheless, while some researchers engage explicitly, and thoroughly, with these ideas, the references are often implicit and not systematically developed. In general, the Weberian legacy remains strong in the study of Pentecostalism, also in relation to other crucial concepts, such as charisma and routinization (Hunt, 2010; Meyer, 2010).

By examining two different although strongly related research fields the aim is to shed light on the shortcomings and strengths of both fields. To build a bridge between Pentecostalism research and the more general research on Protestantism, addressed in this book, we first need to engage with the concept of Protestantism. The historian of religion Helge Årsheim has identified three ways of engaging with the "the protestant" in disciplines such as history, religious studies, theology and the social sciences (Årsheim, 2018 pp. 5–7).

First, there is the definitional approach, where Protestantism is a descriptive tool for identifying a certain current within Christianity. Protestantism is a broad category, often involving everything from the Dutch Reformed Church to Brazilian neo-Pentecostals. These churches have certain doctrinal similarities, but perhaps more importantly they share what they are not; they are not Catholic nor Orthodox.

The second perspective is to discuss Protestantism as an analytical and general common term for Protestant *characteristics*. This line of research traces Protestant characteristics in other religions, as well as how a Protestant form, and understanding, of religion makes itself relevant in society. This could for instance mean exploring how a Protestant understanding of religion has shaped Western educational or legal institutions. Or, linked to this, how Protestantism has become the default religion in many Western institutions, serving as a model for what makes "good religion" or "real religion". Another line of research in this perspective is to explore how religious minorities in Europe or the US adjust to majority communities by adapting Protestant features in their way of doing religion, and another how Protestant missionary religion has had an impact on Buddhism.

Third, Årsheim identifies the perspective that explores Protestantism understood as a broader, cultural current, and examines how Protestantism has led to a series of other wide-ranging societal changes, such as individualism, secularization, democracy and economic growth.

The probably best-known perspective in this line of research has more to do with the Protestant work ethic. The short and popularized understanding of Weber's *The Protestant Ethic and the Spirit of Capitalism* (1905) is that Protestant asceticism was instrumental in creating a modern work ethic, which facilitated the advent of modern capitalism. Exactly this debate, to which extent or how Pentecostal Christianity creates a variation of the "Protestant ethic" has been coined the "key debate" in discussions on Pentecostal economic culture (Robbins, 2004).

Bearing this in mind, what "the Protestant" is and how it affects society is a highly contentious topic. This is particularly a problem in the third category outlined above: the line of research that seeks to ascribe larger societal changes to Protestantism. What is ascribed to Protestantism might in fact have less to do with the religion itself, and more to do with the social and political location of a particular form of Protestantism. It thus becomes very difficult to verify such correlations empirically (Årsheim, 2018 p. 7). Additionally, as much research has pointed out, "Protestantism" is not a precise term: it encompasses a wide variety of different expressions of Christianity, both in form and in time.

As we will see, the three approaches to "the Protestant" are also found in the research on Pentecostalism. Most scholars of Pentecostalism (and scholars of religion in general) are inclined to understand religion as a force in itself, with the ability to shape other areas of society, not just being shaped by society (Lindhardt, 2012, p. 59). The question then becomes, if religion has the ability to transform or reform socio-economic and cultural realities, what are the characteristics of such a change?

The growth of Pentecostalism

In recent decades, the dramatic growth in Pentecostalism in Africa and Latin America has dominated much of the academic focus on religion on the two continents. This movement started slowly at the beginning of the twentieth century, but grew steadily and out of sight of most research. Revivals during the 70s–90s changed the composition of the Pentecostal movement. In addition to poorer populations, the urban, socially upward-mobile middleclass became born-again and joined new independent Pentecostal churches. Prosperity theology and a much more expansive agenda, a strong missionary zeal and a strong impetus to participate actively in society beyond the church inspired these new Pentecostal churches (Lende, 2015).

Traditionally, the birth of the Pentecostal movement is believed to have started with the "outpouring of the spirit" in Azusa Street in the US in 1906, wherefrom it spread to the world. However, with the expansion of Pentecostal studies in Asia, Africa and other continents, this geographical starting point is being questioned, as both Asians and Africans claim that Pentecostal-like movements existed prior to and independently of Azusa Street. Moreover, within Pentecostal circles in the West, there is a shift away from the "miracle" of Azusa Street towards a view that favours a more gradual development of the movement (Anderson, 2010; Kalu, 2008).

Most definitions of Pentecostalism will as a minimum include what is often termed *classical Pentecostalism* (Assemblies of God, Church of God and so on) which had its origin at the beginning of the twentieth century, and *neo-Pentecostalism*, which originated in the 60s and 70s. A broader definition will also include older independent and spirit churches (found in China, India and Sub-Saharan Africa), as well as the Charismatic movement originating in mainline churches from the 60 and on (Anderson, 2010). While institutionally different, the strong and widespread Charismatic revival within mainline Christianity has been so heavily influenced by Pentecostalism that it is often accounted as part of the same broad movement.

In the early 1970s, Pentecostals constituted five percent of global Christianity, today they are closer to 25 per cent. Much of this growth stems from Latin America and Africa. In recent decades, in many African and Latin American countries, Pentecostals have gone from being considered "fanatics" to being mainstream, not just because they have become entangled in "worldly affairs", but more so because the world in which their numbers have grown has become entangled in "Pentecostal affairs" (Lende, 2015).

Research on Pentecostalism

To generalize, we can say that during the first decades of research on Pentecostalism in Latin America and Africa there were two opposing grand narratives: one predicting that Pentecostal growth would have little, or if any, it would be negative, societal impact. The other was that Pentecostalism is a school of democracy with the ability to change individual behaviour to the extent that it changes society (Lende, 2015; Steigenga, 2005, p. 101).

One of the earliest scholars of Pentecostalism outside North America is Lalive D'Epinay who worked with Pentecostals in Chile. He emphasized Pentecostalism as a "haven for the masses", seeing it is a retreat from this world, comprising the poor who through religion revolted against the middle-class and religious establishment (Lalive D'Epinay, 1969). The combination, he argued, of authoritarian structures within the church (the dominant role of the pastor) and the disempowered members would only lead to passivity and submission to the authorities (Lende, 2015, p. 47).

At the same time as D'Epinay published his work, the sociologist and anthropologist Emilio Willems reached another conclusion. He argued that Pentecostals were not passive nor autocratic, and rather accentuated the egalitarianism he found within the movement. He argued that what he saw as key Pentecostal virtues, such as discipline, honesty and sobriety, enabled the poor to advance in society (Willems, 1967). Contrary to D'Epinay, Willems argued that the Pentecostals challenged the traditional social order.

The legacy of these two opposing views, as exemplified by D'Epinay and Willems, is still relevant in the study of Pentecostalism. The 90s saw this in particular through works like David Martin (1990) and Brouwer et al. (Brouwer, 1996). Whereas Martin argued there was a Weberian correlation between Pentecostalism, modernity and social mobility, Brouwer et al. focused on Pentecostalism's conservative and authoritarian aspects, and saw it as an extension of US politics and as the global rise of religious fundamentalism.

Today the literature on Pentecostalism in Latin America and Africa is rich and diverse. Pentecostalism is known for its ability to adapt to local cultures, as well as its striking similarities across cultures and contexts. But despite the almost simultaneous growth of the Pentecostal movement in the two regions, there are relatively few comparative works. Today few scholars attempt to draw larger conclusions, across regions, as to what effect this growth has on the societies where they are flourishing, except for changes in the religious domain.

There are, however, some comparative works examining specific aspects of Pentecostalism, such as globalization (Droogers, 2001; Meyer, 2010), involvement in politics (Adeboye, 2006; Brouwer, 1996; Paul Freston, 2001; Paul Freston, 2008; Ranger, 2008) or Pentecostalism's public engagement. There are numerous important edited volumes with case studies from around the globe (Hefner, 2013;

Wilkinson, 2015), but many refrain from – or refute – the general theories, instead choosing to shed light on diversity and case studies.

One reason for the relative lack of comparative case studies can be explained as a reaction to some failed grand theories on the societal impact of the growth in Pentecostalism. These theories have many ties to the earlier studies of Protestantism.

As research developed, the diversity within this fragmented global movement emerged, and the implications of the growth of Pentecostalism in the two regions was increasingly difficult to measure or prove, which led to the call for careful case studies rather than grand theories (Paul Freston, 2008; Ranger, 2008). Discussing sociological approaches to Pentecostalism, Stephan Hunt describes the difficulties in researching such a multifaceted, fast-changing phenomenon: "Pentecostalism appears to change its colors not only according to wider cultural transformations from modernity to post-modernity but also as a result of dynamics within the movement itself, not the least of all periods of routinization and revivalism" (Hunt, 2010, p. 197). While the legacy of Weber and earlier research on Protestantism and society is important and valuable for the study of Pentecostalism, several scholars have argued for the need to find alternative approaches, to study Pentecostalism as a "first-order project" (Marshall, 2009), not just as a coping mechanism of "something else", for example failed state legitimacy. Others have called for an "expansion of our vocabulary" by focusing on specific features of Pentecostalism, such as its ascetics and style, its use of the body in religious practice, and by exploring the meaning and consequences of the Pentecostal appropriation of the public space and public sphere (Meyer, 2010).

We will explore some of the topics covered in the research literature on Pentecostalism in Africa and Latin America, with a focus on economy, politics and the public sphere. First we will turn to the concept "pentecostalisation", a concept that attempts to capture the specificities of Pentecostal characteristics and impact.

Pentecostalisation

While not as established as the protestantisation concept, the concept *pentecostalisation* made its entrance in academic literature in the early 90s. Pentecostalisation may be used to describe and analyse how Pentecostal beliefs and practices make their presence felt in wider society. Yet, while references to pentecostalisation are relatively common, the concept in itself has no paradigmatic role in academics. More than an elaborated theoretical tool, it is a descriptive and analytical tool, referring to an ongoing, dynamic process through which Pentecostalism gains ground. It is, however, a concept that is good to "think with" as it shifts the emphasis from Pentecostalism as a second-order project, as a supporter of democracy or modernity, to an emphasis on the specific characteristics of Pentecostalism.

A noteworthy exception to the lack of theorizing is Henri Gooren, working in Chile and Latin America, who has initiated a dialogue on how to theorize on the mutual influencing between Pentecostal groups and other societal domains (media, politics, civil society and gender relations and economic attitudes). For Gooren, pentecostalisation is the "[…]combination of Pentecostal numerical growth, Pentecostal influence on other religions, and Pentecostal impact on the rest of society" (Gooren, 2010, p. 356). He hypothesises that there is a logic to what happens when a society is "pentecostalised", but he has yet to dig deeper into how to identify this logic.

Writing on pentecostalisation in the Kenyan and general African context, Damaris Seleina Partisau also highlights numerical strength, influence on other religions (mainly mainline Christianity) and Pentecostal influence on the greater society: "The growth of Pentecostal Christianity is not only in terms of numbers, but also in terms of its increased impact on all aspects of life" (Parsitau, 2007, p. 91).

Precisely this "all aspects of life" is a recurring theme, particularly in countries where Pentecostalism has grown big in number, such as in Kenya, Ghana, Guatemala, Brazil and Nigeria. Writing on Nigeria, Ebenezer Obadare refers to a "pentecostalisation of governance" and states: "In Nigeria, the Pentecostal presence is widely evident; in the sheer explosion of the number of Pentecostal churches; the increasing popularity of the Pentecostal elite; the steady infusion of Pentecostal habits into the fabric of everyday life; the growing popularity of religious spectacles; the transformations of Pentecostal pastors with license to pronounce on love, law and economics; and last but not least, the injection of Pentecostalist forms into popular culture, for instance popular music and Nollywood videos" (Obadare, 2016, p. 78).

In short, pentecostalisation may be used to describe how Pentecostalism is influencing society, including other religious traditions. The diverse work on Pentecostalism and society has many affinities with how the protestantisation literature has evolved, taking as a starting point the three different variations outlined earlier: the Protestant as defining a certain strain of Christianity; the influence of Protestant characteristics on other religions and lastly, the question of how Protestantism has an impact on larger societal developments (Årsheim, 2018). The latter two, influence on other religions and impact on society have also been identified by Gooren, see above. In the following we will look at how these issues are treated in the research on Latin American and African Pentecostalism.

Pentecostalism and the pentecostalisation of religion

Just as defining Protestantism is difficult, defining Pentecostalism is also becoming an increasingly demanding task. As some scholars of Pentecostalism argue, this movement has become so diverse that the term is becoming less and less meaningful

(Robbins, 2004, p. 119). The Pentecostal movement today is global, diverse and constantly changing. Some argue therefore that it is more representative to speak of Pentecostalisms, in the plural, to accentuate both the difference in origins *and* orientation (Anderson, 2010; Bergunder, 2010).

The Pentecostal movement in Africa and Latin America developed in opposition to the established religion in the area, whether this was mainline Protestantism, Catholicism or other Christian traditions. This has led to an uneasy relationship with established religion, where both sides have shared in hostility and suspicion.

Across the research on African and Latin American Pentecostalism there is a consistent focus on how this growth has effected other religions and what some have called "the religious marketplace" in general. Where Pentecostalism has grown to high numbers the pentecostalisation of established religion seems to follow. In the short run, at least, the Pentecostal boom seems to have been good for the overall religious marketplace (Steigenga & Cleary, 2007). But different contexts, both across and within regions have consequences for how Pentecostalism has grown, and also for the research focus. In Latin America the main emphasis has been on the relationship with the dominant Catholic culture and church (Chesnut, 2010; Cleary, 2007; Steigenga & Cleary, 2007). The African context differs due to its more diverse context; being multi-religious as well as multi-confessional.

The Pentecostalisation of other Christians

Research has emphasised how other Christian traditions adapt to, accommodate and imitate Pentecostal characteristics. This focus correlates with the second perspective dominant in the protestantisation literature, outlined at the beginning of this chapter, where research traces typical protestant characteristics in other religions, as well as in other societal institutions (Årsheim, 2018). Yet, while this research traces historical premises in the Protestant legacy on society, the Pentecostal revival is happening "now" and the research focus in Latin American and Africa is on the more immediate consequences for other Christian traditions and religions.

Pentecostalism typically argues that in order to be a true Christian one must be "born again" and make a radical break with the past, whether this might be a Catholic, an Anglican or a non-Christian past. Most of the converts to Pentecostal churches come from the mainline churches, and in many countries, there has been an openly antagonistic relationship with the established churches. In Guatemala, the Catholic Church warned the public of an "invasion of sects" in the 80s, and linked the Pentecostal churches to US cold-war policies. In Nigeria, the main Christian umbrella organization asked the government to curtail the growth of the Pentecostal movement, arguing they feared further growth could lead to a religious war due to the aggressive proselytization in Muslim areas (Lende, 2015, p. 260). The established churches fear both the competition as well as the Pentecostal way of doing religion.

Writing about Kenya, and sub-Saharan Africa more generally, Damaris Parsiatu argues that Pentecostalism has changed the worship and spirituality of mainline Christianity, and states: "More fundamentally, however, Pentecostalisation of African Christianity suggests a theological transformation that informs worship as well as social, public and ecclesial shape and role of Christianity in Africa" (Parsitau, 2007, p. 85). The most evident sign of the pentecostalisation of established Christian traditions is changed worship styles and religious practices: speaking in tongues, healing and Pentecostal worship songs are now found in many established churches across the two regions in question.

The most populous country on the African continent, Nigeria, has experienced strong Pentecostal growth, and is particularly known for its neo-Pentecostal churches and prosperity theology. Several of the Nigerian mega-churches have branches in the other African countries (and even in Latin America). Speaking about the influence of the neo-Pentecostal churches, a Nigerian Baptist pastor summarises much of this as follows:

> Every church in Nigeria has been influenced by the Pentecostal. Every church! Particularly the mainline churches because of what the charismatic groups have been doing, this revival of prayers, beliefs in miracles, you know. A new dimension to ministry, talking prosperity. The churches in the past used old-fashioned auditoriums and seats. Pastors hardly had good cars, they used old-fashioned cars, everything was old-fashioned. But the Pentecostals have a different approach. They believe in prosperity, God has prospered for all. […] So when the mainline [churches] saw that many people were leaving the churches they had to ask themselves: why are they leaving?…we look old-fashioned, it should be redesigned, it should look beautiful, we should bring more flowers, there should be coffee….so: the Pentecostals were doing this and before you know it the mainline churches also were influenced […] None of our mainline churches are the same again! All have been influenced! All! All! (Lende, 2015, pp. 162–163).

In Latin America, the Charismatic movement within the Catholic church has dominated research on the impact of Pentecostalism on other religions (Chesnut, 2003; Cleary, 2011; Thorsen, 2016). This movement is by far the most vibrant and largest Catholic lay movement in Latin America (Cleary, 2011). Spreading since the 1970s, the Charismatic movement has been running an almost parallel institution vis-à-vis the mother church, tolerated but not always embraced by the clerical authorities. The clerical authorities have feared it is too protestant, at times seeing the movement as a bridge towards leaving the church for Pentecostalism. With time the movement now has its clerical supporters, some pragmatic others enthusiastic. While the Catholic Charismatic renewal has its own independent roots and institutions, the movement is analyzed and understood as Pentecostalised Catholicism (Chesnut, 2010; Steigenga & Cleary, 2007).

The Pentecostalisation of Catholicism can be seen in how it influences both how religion is practised and lived for the individual and also for the church as an institution. In terms of religious beliefs and practices for individuals, the Charismatic movement has a strong focus on classic Pentecostal beliefs and practices, such as a concentration on the personal conversion process, speaking in tongues, healing, spiritual warfare, a return to an "enchanted worldview", increased interest in evangelization, and frequent participation in the church. The Catholic Charismatics stress personal commitment rather than cultural identity; they self-identify as the "true Catholic" or "Christian Catholic" and, like Pentecostals, emphasize the need for "a personal encounter with Jesus" and to make lifestyle changes (Thorsen 2012: 258).

The Charismatic movement also resembles the Pentecostals in their willingness to pay for religion (through tithing), the focus on lay leadership and for being a movement that spread from below rather than as an initiative from the top. For the first time in its more than 500-year history on the continent, ordinary people are willing to invest in the Catholic Church through tithing and offerings, and the Charismatic movement is at the forefront of this (Cleary 2011: 262). As with the Pentecostal churches, the Charismatic Church has developed a network of prayer groups and parish communities to provide church-goers with a strong communal network.

Relationship to other religions

Given the prominent presence of Pentecostalism in many areas, non-Christian religions have to relate to it. Particularly in the African context, considerable academic attention is given to the "cultural fit" between traditional religion and Pentecostalism. In fact, precisely Pentecostalism's ability to adapt to local, traditional cultures and religions has been dominant in explaining its global growth. Yet, this adaption is paradoxical as Pentecostals are also known for their war "against their own roots", meaning a frontal attack on traditional religion and culture, whether in African or Latin American contexts (Casanova, 2010, p. 437). In the African context, this paradoxical relationship is often discussed in terms of similarities with African traditional religions when it comes to practices and worldviews, such as miracles, healing, belief in spirits in everyday life and the use of such objects as holy water and oils (M'fundisi-Holloway, 2018).

Similar approaches and findings are found in the work on Latin America, where it is argued that Pentecostalism is "remarkably compatible with the Mayan worldview" (Wilson, 1997, p. 145) and several researchers examine the similarities between for instance Afro-Brazilian religions and Pentecostalism when it comes to ideas and practices on spirit possession. With a comparative view, Andrew Chesnut studied the growth in Pentecostalism, Charismatic Catholicism and African diaspora religions, using case studies from Brazil, Mexico and Guatemala and the term "pneumacentrism", or the centrality of the Spirit or spirits, to highlight the similarities between the three. He argues that in the new religious landscape of Latin America, "liberación" from demonic spirits or exorcism, not liberation from socioeconomic inequalities is the dominant trend. This process was so strong in the 1980s in many Latin American countries that "such was the consumer demand for pneumatic spirituality, that if religious specialties did not produce it, their churches faced stagnation and even decline" (Chestnut 2003: 78).

Pentecostalism has experienced growth at the expense of traditional religions and established Christianity. But research has also accentuated the possibility that the growth of Pentecostalism has also been beneficial for competing religions as Pentecostals have created a consumer demand for spiritual goods, which other religious producers also can offer (Chesnut, 2003). However, in the research on Latin America the growth of Pentecostalism is also discussed in relation to secularization. An increasing number of second-generation Pentecostals, as in the case of Mexico (Steigenga & Cleary, 2007), seem to leave Pentecostals churches without entering other religious communities. These debates are influenced to a high degree by similar debates on Protestantism and secularism.

A recent and more marginal phenomenon is the focus on the pentecostalisation of non-traditional and non-Christian religions, prominently Islam. While discussed in other countries, such as Kenya (Parsitau, 2007, p. 90), this features most prominently in examples from Nigeria, and in particular the Nigeria-originated NASFAT (Adetona, 2012; Obadare, 2016; Soares, 2009).

The Nasrul-Lahi-L-Fatih Soceity of Nigeria (NASFAT) started as prayer group in 1995 and is today one of the stronger muslim movements operating in Nigeria. They attract young, urban upwardly mobile Muslims, particulalry in south-west Nigeria. They are characterized by their long prayer meetings, Friday vigils, a focus on healing and on economic empowerment, socio-political engagement, education and missionary activities; all activites that are also at the core of Pentecostalism. While NASFAT emerged due to many factors, such as ongoing reformations within Islam, the Pentecostal influence has been identified both by researchers and by people within the movement (Obadare, 2016; Sengupta, 2003). This Pentecostal influence is seen in both religious practice and modus operandi. Obadare sums it up in this way:

> I use "Charismatic Islam" to articulate the visibility within this "new" Islam of practices, modes of worship and proselytizing, organizational features, and repertoires of devo-

tion and prayer that closely resembles the forms and expressions normally exclusively associated with Pentecostal Christianity in Nigeria (Obadare, 2016, p. 76).

In style and visibility, NASFAT resembles Pentecostal churches that have appropriated the secular urban space, such as sport stadiums, concert halls and cinemas for their churches; as NASFAT's popularity grew rapidly and already in the late 90s they were filling sports stadiums in Lagos for their prayer meetings. While prayer is crucial to Muslim practice, the way prayer is done in NASFAT resembles Pentecostal prayers. There is a growing popularity in "all-night prayer sessions", "prayer cells" and "prayer warriors".. The substance of the prayers has also changed, for instance with an emphasis on such supernatural forces as evil and the occult (Obadare, 2016, p. 86).

This can possibly be understood in relation to the increased focus on the demonic in the Nigerian and Sub-Saharan context, where the emergence of Pentecostalism in the public sphere has led to an obsession with the occult, a language and a theme adopted by non-Pentecostal actors (Rosalind Hackett, 2003; Rosalind Hackett, 2012).

Pentecostalisation of society

Although in different forms, many Latin American and African countries experienced democratization as well as economic liberalization in the 1980s and 90s. The explosive growth of Pentecostal churches occurred in the same period, aided by these structural conditions. The liberalization of the media, the economy and the public space opened the door for the newcomers, the Pentecostals. Thus, Pentecostalism is in some sense a product *of* democracy, but whether it is also a potential *for* democracy is much less certain (Paul Freston, 2008, p. 17).

Parts of the study of Protestantism have been ripe with assertions of Protestantism's positive influence on the development of everything from modernity to human rights and democracy (Årsheim, 2018 p. 7). The study of Pentecostalism has been more cautious despite a few grand-scale theories that have been difficult to verify empirically.

In the following, we will examine three important aspects of the research on Pentecostalism and society across Africa and Latin America: 1) how Pentecostalism engages with the economy, 2) how it relates to politics, and finally, 3) how Pentecostalism goes public. While the two first topics, the economy and politics, relate directly to questions also posed in the research on Protestantism (Årsheim, 2018), the third topic relating to the public sphere has carved out its own independent research agenda. But just as the research that explores large-scale societal effects of Protestantism has been strongly criticized for not being able to verify claims of

Protestantism's alleged influence on the economy, modernity or democracy, similar criticism from researchers of Pentecostalism have been refuted.

Pentecostalisation of the economy

As outlined, the question as to whether the growth of Pentecostalism leads to a variant of a Weberian upward social and economic mobility is important in the research on Pentecostalism. Yet, ever since empirical case studies started to take precedence, the large-scale claims are frequently challenged as "the available evidence is scarce and contradictory" (Gooren, 2010, p. 363) and several studies indicated that "we just do not know" when it comes to such questions as whether individuals or communities see an increase in their economic status (Drønen, 2012 p. 334).

Another reason the economic and social-mobility thesis was stronger earlier was the character of the classical Pentecostal movement; hard work ethic, strong moral codes and abstinence from alcohol and adultery echoed the Dutch puritans in Weber's case. With the advent of neo-Pentecostalism and prosperity theology, many lost sight of this connection. The sociologist Peter Berger, for instance, still argued that Pentecostalism – in its classical form – was able to create alternative networks characterized by such virtues as personal integrity, honesty and hard work, enabling them to prosper economically and socially in society. He did not see neo-Pentecostalism carrying the same potential (Berger, 2010). Neo-Pentecostalism has been, and is, particularly strong in many of the emerging mega-cities in the sub-Saharan Africa, which is one (of several) reasons why many scholars of African Pentecostalism dispute this connection (Gifford, 2004; Nogueira-Godsey, 2011).

However, the questions are still important. A different approach to the topic is the contribution of Dena Freeman and colleagues (Freeman, 2012) who examine the Weberian connection through a focused, empirical approach, comparing the impact of Pentecostal churches on development and societal change with the professional secular NGOs working on development. Freeman finds that Pentecostals are often more effective that secular NGOs as change agents, arguing that Pentecostals have adapted better to the neo-liberal economy. While she is careful to warn against a repetition of Weber's thesis on the connection between sixteenth century European Calvinists and the development of late modern Pentecostalism in Africa today – due to differences in historical context, type of capitalism and type of Protestantism – she still thinks there are certain similarities worth exploring. This relates in particular to how Pentecostals, as with Weber's Calvinists, stimulate new behaviour. She writes: "[Pentecostalism] is a form of Protestantism that not only fits with African sensibilities, but also stimulates a transformation of behavior that can lead to success, or at least upward mobility, in the contemporary neo-liberal economy. It motivates new behavior and renders them moral" (Freeman, 2012, p. 20). This ability to change behaviour is also one of the main reasons why she argues that secular NGOs fail, comparatively to Pentecostals, to change people's lives.

The connection between the neo-liberal economy and Pentecostalism is multifaceted and an important topic in the literature, where the main argument is that there is a strong consonance, or fit, between the spread of the neo-liberal economy and neo-Pentecostalism (Meyer, 2007, 2010). Meyer argues here, as several others do, that while Weber's concepts and theories can be inspiring for our study, his observations about the Calvinist should not be used as a blueprint for Pentecostalism. One reason, alongside the apparent different characteristics of the movement, is the argument put forward by many scholars that the correlation is not present due to the difficulty of comparing extremely different socio-economic contexts: pre-industrial Europe and modern day Latin America and Africa (Gifford, 2004).

The Pentecostals, particularly in their neo-Pentecostal form, challenge the way we understand religion and the economy. Prosperity theology has given rise to the mega-rich pastors flying in private jets as well as to a theology that explicitly pursues material wellbeing here on earth. Their explicit ethos of economic progress, apparent in the teachings of but also in the activities organized by the churches, may be the key in a world where the path to prosperity is more through private entrepreneurship than employment.

While most research will refrain from making explicit connections between growth of Pentecostalism in Latin America and Africa and major socio-economic progress, the focus on the economy is central to the study of Pentecostalism. The question centres around whether Pentecostalism reflects, reinforces or reforms socio-economic realities.

Pentecostalisation of politics

Turning to comparative questions regarding Pentecostalism's political potential, the answers are also inconclusive and contradictory. The democratization processes across Latin America and Africa in the 1980s and 90s coincided with the explosion of Pentecostalism, and this new movement's ability to foster a democratic political culture is key in many of the comparative studies as well as specific case studies (Bjune, 2016; Paul Freston, 2008, 2010; Kolapo, 2018; Marshall, 2009; Obadare, 2006; Ranger, 2008; Steigenga & Cleary, 2007).

While explicitly apolitical in its earlier days, the Pentecostals have been explicitly political for decades now. Across the two regions, Pentecostal political parties have been founded, Pentecostal pastors run for president, Pentecostal media stations actively discuss politics and Pentecostals take to the streets in demonstrations, actively showing their various opinions on national issues. Yet, because the Pentecostal movement is inherently fragmented in nature, a common political Pentecostal political ideology has been difficult to detect across cases and regions. In addition, different contexts encourage different types of political action. There is, however, a clear tendency in several countries, most evident in Latin America, where the left-right political spectrum is clearer: conservative theology translates into conservative politics.

For many researchers, however, Pentecostals' political potential does not necessarily lie in their explicit political engagement, but rather indirectly as associations in civil society, providing new social spaces and skills for the poor and marginalized, creating a platform or avenue for change (1990). Nevertheless, others argue that these overtly positive pronouncements on Pentecostalism's democratic potential rest on a theory-driven and simplistic understanding of what the role of civil society might be (Steigenga, 2005, p. 101). Less discussed are the actual realities of the African and Latin American states, several of them characterized by neo-liberal policies, corruption and mismanagement. While we might often employ idealized theoretical understandings of "civil society" in our analysis, this may be as equally true for our understanding of how the state works. African and Latin American states in the twenty-first century function quite differently from several of our theoretical notions of how a state should work. Studying the Pentecostal movement as a first-order project, a pragmatic and adaptable movement growing in the midst of democratic state formation gives us valuable insights into where power is located in society. Where Pentecostals have grown to large numbers they have sought political influence, but equally important is their impact on education, the economy and the public sphere, to mention some of the most important areas (Lende, 2015). Rather than being characterized as voluntary associations within the state, they can also be seen as alternative spaces outside, or parallel, to the state.

An interesting turn in the study of politics and Pentecostalism has been to move away from the question of party politics and voting patterns and rather look at how Pentecostals do politics, more on their own terms. Identifying how and where Pentecostals locate power in society is one way of attempting to understand Pentecostal politics. Ruth Marshall, working on Africa, talks of "Pentecostal political spiritualties" which she claims "stubbornly resist the distinction between the sacred and the secular" (Marshall, 2009, p. 3). She argues that Pentecostals do politics through such approaches as spiritual warfare against demons of corruption or by occupying the public space with posters and music. Ebenezer Obadare talks of a "pentecostalisation of governance" where the political and public spaces in Nigeria are filled with prophecies, spiritual warfare and networks of wealthy Pentecostals and politicians, "the Lagos/Ibadan theocratic class" (Obadare, 2006). While explicit politics is also increasingly important for many Pentecostal individuals or institutions, tracing how Pentecostals perform politically, in unconventional ways, has aided our understanding of Pentecostalism. This more grounded approach is indebted to, among other disciplines, anthropological research which has bypassed much of the secularity impasse present in studies of religion and politics, studying the people in religious movements – particularly Islam – in their everyday personal and public lives.

Pentecostalisation of the public sphere

One of the most salient characteristics of Pentecostalism is how it radically differs from the mainline religions in its engagement with the public sphere (Adeboye, 2006; Englund, 2011; Rosalind Hackett, 2012; Meyer, 2011; O'Neill, 2010; Parsitau, 2007). Research, particularly on the neo-Pentecostal movement, has thoroughly discussed new manners of going public in African and Latin America. While they use and have a presence on television, the internet and radio, Pentecostals importantly also occupy *public space* through billboards, merchandising, music and churches. Visibility is a key characteristic of Pentecostalism, particularly in its neo-Pentecostal form.

This research on the Pentecostal public presence points out several characteristics of the Pentecostal movement beyond mere descriptive purposes. Across the two regions, research has shown at least two very important aspects of how Pentecostalism affects societies. First, through being strongly present in the public sphere Pentecostals have the ability to influence topics in the public discourse. This has led to what might be called a moralization of the public sphere, or "sacralising of the public" (Meyer, 2011).

Secondly, its presence in the public sphere is also a stepping-stone to other arenas, such as politics. When a Brazilian megachurch pastor supports a political candidate in the national elections it is not just his support that it is gained, but also the media outlets belonging to the church, which will also be used for campaigning. The presence in the public spheres of the emerging and struggling democracies of Africa and Latin America may translate into power also in other areas of society.

Conclusion

A general legacy for scholars of religion is that the processes of societal change can come from the religious sphere, that religion in itself might be transformative, for the individual, and possibly therefore also for society. But until now, our models have provided us with contradictory findings on the major comparative questions regarding Pentecostalism's possibility to transform economic and political culture. Just as it has been difficult to find empirical support for general theories concerning established Protestantism's impact on modernity, democracy and modern capitalism, so have the same inquiries regarding Pentecostalism led to inconclusive answers. A rather obvious answer would be that context matters, and Pentecostalism will have different types of impact in different contexts. Yet, the growth and the characteristics of Pentecostalism in Africa and Latin America are remarkably similar. Is the movement a mere *reflection* of new political and socio-economic realities or does the movement also have the possibility to *transform* societies? Future research needs to address these questions, preferably also with comparative case studies.

The research on Pentecostalism has benefitted from the older questions dominating research on Protestantism, but it has been necessary to find its own vocabulary and questions more suited to both the movement's characteristics as well as our contemporary context. Focusing on the particularities of Pentecostal growth in its various locations has been necessary. However, given the spectacular similarities of Pentecostal growth across the region, new comparative studies must also embark on a journey through the more general questions.

Bibliography

Adeboye, O. (2006). Pentecostal Challenges in Africa and Latin America: A comparative foucs on Brazil and Nigeria *Africa Zamani, 11*, 136–159.

Anderson, A. (2010). Varieties, Taxonomies, and Definitions. In A. Anderson, M. Bergunder, A. F. Droogers, & C. van der Laan (eds.), *Studying global Pentecostalism: Theories and methods* (pp. 13–29). Berkeley: University of California Press.

Berger, P. L. (2010). Max Weber is alive and well, and living in Guatemala: The Protestant ethic of today *The Review of Fatih & International Affairs, 8*(4), 3–9.

Bergunder, M. (2010). The Cultural Turn. In A. Anderson, M. Bergunder, A. F. Droogers, & C. van der Laan (eds.), *Studying global Pentecostalism: Theories and methods*, (pp. 51–73). Berkeley: University of California Press.

Bjune, M. C. (2016). *Religious change and political continuity. The evangelical church in Guatemalan politics*. Dissertation, University of Bergen.

Brouwer, G. a. R. (1996). *Exporting the American Gospel. Global Christian Fundamentalism* New York: Routledge.

Casanova, J. (2010). Religion Challenging the Myth of Secular Democracy. In L. Christoffersen, H. Petersen, & S. S. Ali (eds.), *Religion in the 21st century: challenges and transformations* (pp. 19–36). Farnham: Ashgate.

Chesnut, R. A. (2003). *Competitive Spirits: Latin America's New Religious Economy*. New York: Oxford University Press.

Chesnut, R. A. (2010). Conservative Christian Competitors: Pentecostals and Charismatic Catholics in Latin America's New Religious Economy. *SAIS Review, 30*(1), 91–103.

Cleary, E. L. (2007). The Catholic Charismatic Renewal. In T. J. Steigenga & E. L. Cleary (eds.), *Conversion of a Continent: Contemporary Religious Change in Latin America* (pp. 153–173). New Brunswick: Rutgers University Press.

Cleary, E. L. (2011). *The Rise of Charismatic Catholicism in Latin America*. Gainesville: University Press of Florida.

Droogers, A. F. (2001). Globalisation and Pentecostal Success. In A. C. a. R. Marshall-Fratani (ed.), *Between Babel and Pentecost: Transnational Pentecostalism in Latin America and Africa* (pp. 41-61). Bloomington: IUP.

Drønen, T. S. (2012). Weber, Prosperity and the Protestant Ethic: Some Reflections on Pentecostalism and Economic Development. *Swedish Missiological Themes, 100*(3), 321-335.

Englund, H. (2011). *Christianity and public culture in Africa* (Vol. 14). Ohio University Press.

Freeman, D. (2012). *Pentecostalism and development: churches, NGOs and social change in Africa*. Basingstoke: Palgrave Macmillan. The Van Leer Jerusalem Institute.

Freston, P. (2001). *Evangelicals and Politics in Asia, Africa and Latin America*. Cambridge: Cambridge University Press.

Freston, P. (2008). *Evangelical Christianity and Democracy in Latin America*. Oxford University Press.

Freston, P. (2010). Researching the Heartland of Pentecostalism: Latin Americans at Home and Abroad. *Fieldwork in Religion, 3*(2), 122-144.

Gifford, P. (2004). *Ghana's new Christianity: pentecostalism in a globalising African economy*. London: Hurst.

Gooren, H. (2010). The Pentecostalization of Religion and Society in Latin America. *Exchange, 39*(4), 355-376. doi:doi:https://doi.org/10.1163/157254310X537025

Hackett, R. (2003). Discourses of the Demonization in Africa and Beyond. *Diogenes, 50*(3), 61-75.

Hackett, R. (2012). Devil Bustin'satellites: How media liberalization in Africa generates religious intolerance and conflict. In D. Smith (ed.), *The religious dimensions of conflict and peace in a neoliberal Africa. Notre Dame: University of Notre Dame Press. Google Scholar* (pp. 163-208): University of Notre Dame Press.

Hefner, R. W. (ed.) (2013). *Global Pentecostalism in the 21st Century*. Indiana Indiana Univeristy Press.

Hunt, S. (2010). Sociology of Religion. In A. e. a. Anderson (ed.), *Studying Global Pentecostalism. Theories + Methods*. Berkeley: Univeristy of California Press.

Kalu, O. (2008). *African Pentecostalism: an introduction*. Oxford: Oxford University Press.

Kolapo, F. J. (2018). Political Ramifications of Some Shifts in Nigeria's Pentecostal Movement. In A. Afolayan, O. Yacob-Haliso, & T. Falola (eds.), *Pentecostalism and Politics in Africa* (pp. 245-275). Cham: Springer International Publishing.

Lalive D'Epinay, C. (1969). *Haven of the Masses: A study of the Pentecostal movement in Chile*. London: Lutterworth Press.

Lende, G. (2015). *The rise of Pentecostal power: exploring the politics of Pentecostal growth in Nigeria and Guatemala*. Det teologiske menighetsfakultet, Oslo.

Lindhardt, M. (2012). Pentecostalism and Politics in Neoliberal Chile. *Iberoamericana. Nordic Journal of Latin American and Caribbean studies, XLII*(1-2), 59-83.

M'fundisi-Holloway, N. (2018). When Pentecostalism meets African Ingidenous Religions: Conflict, Compromise, or Incorporation? In A. A. Afolayan, O. Yacob-Haliso, & T. Falola (eds.), *Pentecostalism and Politics in Africa* (pp. 87–100). Blacksburg Palgrave Macmillian.

Marshall, R. (2009). *Political Spiritualities. The Pentecostal Revolution in Nigeria* Chicago: The University of Chicago Press.

Martin, D. (1990). *Tongues of fire the explosion of Protestantism in Latin America*. Oxford Blackwell.

Meyer, B. (2007). Pentecostalism and neo-liberal capitalism: faith, prosperity and vision in African pentecostal-charismatic churches. *Journal for the Study of Religion, 20*(2), 5–28.

Meyer, B. (2010). Pentecostalism and Globalization. In M. Bergunder, A. F. Droogers, C. v. d. Laan, & A. Anderson (eds.), *Studying global Pentecostalism: Theories and methods*. Berkeley: University of California Press.

Meyer, B. (2011). Going and making public. Some reflections on pentecostalism as public religion in Ghana. In H. Englund (ed.), *Christianity and Public Culture in Africa* (pp. 149–166). Columbus: Ohio University Press.

Nogueira-Godsey, P. G. (2011). The Protestant Ethic and and African Pentecostalism: A case study. *Journal for the Study of Religion, 24*(1), 5–22.

O'Neill, K. L. (2010). *City of God: Christian citizenship in postwar Guatemala* (Vol. 7): University of California Press.

Obadare, E. (2006). Pentecostal Presidency? The Lagos-Ibadan 'Theocratic Class'& the Muslim 'Other'. *Review of African Political Economy, 33*(110), 665–678.

Obadare, E. (2016). The Muslim response to the Pentecostal surge in Nigeria: Prayer and the rise of charismatic Islam. *Journal of Religious and Political Practice, 2*(1), 75–91. doi:10.1080/20566093.2016.1085240

Parsitau, D. S. (2007). From the periphery to the centre: the Pentecostalisation of mainline Christianity in Kenya. *Missionalia : Southern African Journal of Mission Studies, 35*(3), 83–111.

Ranger, T. O. (2008). *Evangelical Christianity and democracy in Africa*: OUP USA.

Robbins, J. (2004). The Globalization of Pentecostal and Charismatic Christianity. *Annual Review of Antropology, 33*, 117–143.

Sengupta, S. a. R., Larry (2003). Where faith grows, fired by Pentecostalism. *New York Times*. Retrieved from http://www.nytimes.com/2003/10/14/world/where-faith-grows-fired-by-pentecostalism.html

Soares, B. (2009). An Islamic Social Movement In Contemporary West Africa: Nasfat Of Nigeria. *Movers and Shakers* (pp. 178–196): Brill. Retrieved from http://booksandjournals.brillonline.com/content/books/10.1163/ej.9789004180130.i-260.73. doi:doi:https://doi.org/10.1163/ej.9789004180130.i-260.73

Steigenga, T. J. (2005). Democracia y el crecimineto del protestantismo evangélico en Guatemala: entendiendo la complejidad política de la religión "pentecostalisada". *América Latina Hoy, 41*, 99–119.

Steigenga, T. J., & Cleary, E. L. (2007). *Conversion of a Continent: Contemporary Religious Change in Latin America*. New Brunswick, N.J.: Rutgers University Press.

Thorsen, J. E. (2016). The Catholic Charismatic Renewal and the Incipient Pentecostalization of Latin American Catholicism. In V. Garrard-Burnett, P. Freston, & S. C. Dove (eds.), *The Cambridge History of Religions in Latin America* (pp. 462–479).

Wilkinson, M. (2015). The Emergence, Development and Pluralisation of Global Pentecostalism In S. Hunt (Ed.), *Handbook of global contemporary Christianity: themes and developments in culture, politics, and society* (Vol. Vol. 10, pp. 93–112). Leiden: Brill.

Willems, E. (1967). *Followers of the Faith: Culture Change and the Rise of Protestantism in Brazil and Chile*. Nashville: Vanderbilt University Press.

Wilson, E. (1997). Guatemalan Pentecostals: Something on their Own. In E. C. a. H. Stewart-Gambino (Ed.), *Power, Politics and Pentecostals in Latin America* (pp. 139–162). Boulder, CO: Westview Press.

Årsheim, H. (2018). Protestantisering og protestantisme: Kilden til demokratisering, økonomisk utvikling og rettslig orden? *Kirke og kultur. Religion og samfunn, 123*(1), 16–33.

Karin Neutel

Chapter 4: Requiring Religious Motivations

Reflections on the Norwegian Law on Circumcision

1. Introduction

In recent years the circumcision of boys has been a topic of political and public debate in several European countries. Proposals have been put forward to ban circumcision, to set a minimum age for boys to be circumcised, or to restrict by whom and how the operation can be performed.[1] In Sweden (2001), Germany (2012), and Norway (2014), these debates resulted in new legislation intended to regulate the practice and impose certain medical requirements.[2] This chapter will reflect on the Norwegian law, and will examine some of the implications of its formulation in connection with a Protestant framing of circumcision.

In its European context, the Norwegian law is exceptional due to the way it describes the circumcision in question. Its full title is 'Law on Ritual Circumcision of Boys' ('Lov om rituell omskjæring av gutter' LOV-2014-06-20-40), and defines ritual circumcision as 'a surgical procedure whereby the foreskin of the penis is entirely or partially removed, and where the purpose is religiously motivated', or 'religiously justified' ('religiøst begrunnet').[3] In contrast, the Swedish and German laws both define the circumcision of boys according to what it is not, namely not medically grounded ('som inte anses utgöra hälso - och sjukvård', 'eine medizinisch nicht erforderliche Beschneidung des nicht einsichts - und urteilsfähigen männlichen Kindes'). Neither the Swedish nor the German legislation further

---

1 For a discussion of the legal situation in the UK, Germany, the Netherlands, and the Nordic countries, see Esther I. J. Erlings, 'The Law and Practices of Ritual Male Circumcision: Time for Review', in Sibnath Deb (Ed.), *Child Safety, Welfare and Well-being: Issues and Challenges* (New Delhi: Springer 2016), 95–113; Mark Swatek-Evenstein, 'Limits of Enlightenment and the Law: On the Legality of Ritual Male Circumcision in Europe Today', *Merkourios* 29/77 (2013): 42–50; Johanna Schiratzki, 'Banning God's Law in the Name of The Holy Body: The Nordic Position on Ritual Male Circumcision', *The Family in Law* 5 (2011): 35–53.
2 The full text of the Swedish, 'Lag (2001:499) om omskärelse av pojkar', can be accessed here https://www.riksdagen.se/sv/dokument-lagar/dokument/svensk-forfattningssamling/lag-2001499-om-omskarelse-av-pojkar_sfs-2001-499; The German law, '§ 1631 d Abs. 1 BGB', can be found at https://dejure.org/gesetze/BGB/1631d.html.
3 LOV-2014-06-20-40, § 2.Definisjon av rituell omskjæring 'Med rituell omskjæring menes i denne lov et kirurgisk inngrep hvor forhud rundt penis fjernes helt eller delvis, og hvor formålet er religiøst begrunnet.' The full text of the law is available at https://lovdata.no/dokument/NL/lov/2014-06-20-40.

qualifies the nature of the procedure as either ritual or religious, nor specifies any requirements regarding the motivations for which it is undertaken.

The only reference to religion in the Swedish and German legislation occurs in relation to allowing religious specialists who are not medical doctors to perform circumcision, in the Swedish case during the first two months after birth, in the German law during the first six months.[4] These specialists are described in both instances as being connected to a 'religious community', in the Swedish case further specified as a religious community 'where circumcision is included as part of a religious tradition' (in Swedish 'den som föreslagits av ett trossamfund där omskärelse ingår som en del i en religiös tradition'; the German wording here is 'von einer Religionsgesellschaft dazu vorgesehene Personen'). It is thus only for determining who can perform circumcision, in making an exception for a non-medical, religious specialist – in practice most likely a Jewish *mohel*, who would circumcise on the eighth day, although this is not specified and the time frames do not directly reflect this – that religion is mentioned in the Swedish and German regulations on circumcision, not in connection with the motivations for the circumcision as such.

Although the Norwegian law has so far not been tested in court, it invites further reflection on its chosen formulation, especially given the problematic nature of 'religion' as a category in legal thought. This paper will explore some of the potential complications that arise from this particular aspect of the Norwegian law relating to the circumcision of boys. It will examine the problems associated with the concept of 'religion' within the law in relation to circumcision, and the implications of two recent rulings on cases related to circumcision in Germany. My focus and interest in the context of this volume lies not predominantly in the field of law, but rather

---

4 Lag (2001:499) om omskärelse av pojkar, 6 § determines that while after the age of two months, no person who is not a registered physician may not perform a circumcision, before that age, special permission may be issued to someone 'who is proposed by a religious community where circumcision is included as part of a religious tradition, if the person has the competence as prescribed under section 11, is deemed to be able to carry out the procedure according to the requirements that apply to the procedure and otherwise is competent to perform circumcision' ('Annan person än legitimerad läkare får inte utföra omskärelse på pojkar som är äldre än två månader. Särskilt tillstånd att utföra omskärelse får meddelas den som föreslagits av ett trossamfund där omskärelse ingår som en del i en religiös tradition, om personen har den kompetens som föreskrivs med stöd av 11 §, bedöms kunna utföra ingreppet i enlighet med de krav som gäller för ingreppet och i övrigt är lämplig att utföra omskärelser.'). § 1631 d Abs. 1 BGB specifies in paragraph 2 that during the first six months after birth, 'persons designated by a religious community may also perform circumcisions in accordance with paragraph 1, provided that they are specifically trained and equally capable of practicing circumcision, without being a doctor.' ('In den ersten sechs Monaten nach der Geburt des Kindes dürfen auch von einer Religionsgesellschaft dazu vorgesehene Personen Beschneidungen gemäß Absatz 1 durchführen, wenn sie dafür besonders ausgebildet und, ohne Arzt zu sein, für die Durchführung der Beschneidung vergleichbar befähigt sind').

in that of religion, specifically cultural perceptions of male circumcision in light of possible Protestant perspectives.

2. Religion, law and circumcision

2.1 Problems with defining religion in legal contexts

There are many problems associated with defining religion, both in general and specifically in relation to legal contexts (Idinopulos and Wilson, 1998; Platvoet and Molendijk, 1999; Sullivan, 2005). Being aware of these problems is important since defining religion is an exercise of power that can have serious repercussions for those who are included or excluded under any given definition (Aldridge, 2013: 22; Sandberg, 2014: 29). This is especially true for legal definitions of religion which, as Russell Sandberg observes, invariably make very real differences in people's lives (Sandberg, 2014: 39; Gunn, 2003: 191). Legal understandings of religion either explicitly or implicitly 'determine which individuals and groups should be bestowed with legal advantages by virtue of the fact that they are "religious"' (Sandberg, 2014: 30). In the case of the Norwegian law relating to circumcision, the presence of the term 'religious' thus invites uncertainty about who is included or excluded, who is given legal advantage and who is denied this legitimacy.

Sandberg distinguishes five partly overlapping problems of defining 'religion', the first three of which are particularly relevant here. The first is the multiplicity of definitions of religion, which means that a lexical or universal definition, which gives the customary meaning of the word, is almost impossible to find. Instead, in a legal context, the problem of defining religion should be understood as finding a stipulative definition, one that is not all encompassing, but rather 'fulfils the specific purpose of the legislator', where this purpose and the context of the definition are made explicit (Sandberg, 2014: 32; Sandberg, 2018: 132–157).

The second problem is religious pluralism and diversity, which make it difficult to determine who and what is or is not religious. Yet as Sandberg notes, this makes awareness of how boundaries are drawn increasingly important, since 'evaluating new forms of religious behaviour by reference to forms of religion previously protected runs the risk of excluding those that fall outside the mainstream' (2014: 33).

The third problem identified by Sandberg is that 'religion' as such is a 'Western' category which has no necessary equivalent in other parts of the world. For Sandberg, acknowledging the key role of Western understandings of religion does not mean that defining religion is impossible or misguided, but rather 'points to an appreciation which should inform the attempt to define'.[5]

This third point is of course particularly relevant in the context of this volume, especially in connection with the first two. The fact that religion is such a complex and diverse phenomenon which is difficult to grasp is at least in part due to the fact that the concept stems from a Western Christian model, which other practices, ideas and so on are made to fit. Daniel Dubuisson describes the concept of religion as 'the legitimate daughter of Christianity' (2003: 9).[6] The nature and definition, origins and expression of what is seen as religious 'were born in the West' (2003: 9). Tomoko Masuzawa has further shown how the idea of 'world religions' was closely tied up with the idea of Christianity as the true religion (2005). This idea developed in missionary and colonial encounters and religion-making functioned as a tool of colonial and neo-colonial governance (Laborde, 2014). What is or is not counted as religious – but rather as traditional, or national, for example – is thus always also a political move.

An important aspect of the Christian bias inherent in many of the definitions that are given is that religion tends to be seen as a matter of internal convictions, as individual belief primarily, rather than as a more collective or lived phenomenon (e. g., King, 2011: 49–50; Jakobsen, 2014: 215–217). Such an understanding of religion relies on the particularly Protestant Christian assumption that faith is the essence not only of Christian religion, but of religion in general. This tendency is also evident in understandings of religion that occur in legal contexts, both explicitly and implicitly.[7] The German Federal Administrative Court, for example, defines religion as 'any specific certainty as regards the whole of the world and the origin and purpose of mankind which gives sense to human life and the world, and which transcends the world' (European Commission, Directorate-General for Employment, Social Affairs and Inclusion, 2007: 27). Religion understood as a 'certainty' about the 'purpose of mankind' becomes a remarkably cognitive phenomenon. Stephen Feldman similarly shows that freedom of religion as upheld by the United States Supreme Court is skewed towards a Christian, especially

---

[5] The final two problems discussed by Sandberg are the 'indescribable essence' of religion and the contention that 'religion as studied by scholars is qualitatively different from the religious activities that actually occur in society' (Sandberg, 2014: 34–37).

[6] I have discussed this Christian origin in relation to circumcision in Karin Neutel, 'Shedding Religious Skin: An Intersectional Analysis of the Claim that Male Circumcision Limits Religious Freedom', In: Valérie Nicolet Anderson and Marianne Bjelland Kartzow (eds.), *The Complexity of Conversion: Intersectional Perspectives on Religious Change in Antiquity and Beyond* (Sheffield: Equinox, 2021). On the Christian origins of the concept of religion see also Nongbri, 2013; Tambiah, 1990; Dressler and Mandair, 2011; Lindkvist, 2013: 429–447; Nurser, 2003: 841–881.

[7] On this bias in a legal context, see Woodhead, 2011: 121–143 and Gunn, 2003: 189–215.

Protestant understanding of religion, in that it is seen as focused on faith rather than action and as individual rather than collective. This concept of freedom of religion, he argues, has primarily been developed out of a Protestant idea of freedom of conscience (2000: 262–266).

The tenacity of belief as the primary reference point for religion can be seen in recent legal discourse in the pairing of 'religion and belief'. In this pair, 'belief' refers to non-religious (or not necessarily religious) convictions, which are seen to deserve protection similar to religion. Yvonne Sherwood has recently traced the remarkable historical development of the terms religion and belief, and analysed the implications of their contemporary pairing in a legal setting (2015). Even though the addition of 'belief' to 'religion' seems intended to show 'religion' its place, and underline the importance of its negation, belief understood as the secular cognate of religion paradoxically suggests that religion is in fact the reference point and guardian for what counts as secular belief. In order to merit protection, belief 'must meet the high entrance requirements set by religion', which are formed by its presumed seriousness, cohesion, and importance (Sherwood, 2015: 33). For Sherwood, the move to elevate 'belief' ignores the endeavours of religious scholars discussed above to distinguish it from religion, and to relegate belief to the side-lines as a 'Christian and colonial imposition' (2015: 34).

Elizabeth Shakman Hurd (2012) also expresses criticism of the tendency in law to equate religion and belief. If those who advocate religious freedom focus particularly on the freedom to believe, she suggests, they will 'privilege particular kinds of religious subjectivity while disabling others. They contribute to the normalization of (religious) subjects for whom believing (…) is taken as *the* universal defining characteristic of what it means to be religious, and the right to believe as the essence of what it means to be free, excluding other modes of living in the world, as bodies in communities to which they are obliged, without attention to individual "belief"'. In the context of circumcision, Shakman Hurd's warning about the way bodies are seen to relate to religion is of course of particular relevance.

In discussing the complexity of religion in relation to law on religion-based asylum claims, Jeremy Gunn distinguishes two other ways of seeing 'religion' that are excluded when it is narrowed only to belief: 'religion as identity', and 'religion as way of life' (2003: 200–205). While religion as belief emphasises doctrines and ideas, religion as identity emphasises affiliation with a group. In this sense, religion as identity is experienced as something similar to family, ethnicity, race, or nationality. Religion as identity can therefore be something into which people are born rather than something to which they convert after a process of study, prayer, or reflection (Gunn, 2003: 201).

Seeing religion as a 'way of life' means for Gunn that it is 'associated with actions, rituals, customs, and traditions that may distinguish the believer from adherents of other religions' (2003: 204). In this view, rituals are not outward, and secondary, expressions of a primary internal conviction, as the Norwegian law appears to assume – and which is a common assumption in the Norwegian debate on circumcision, as Vebjørn Horsfjord shows in this volume – but rather constitutive of religious life itself.

2.2 Religious motivations and circumcision

By stipulating that circumcision requires religious motivations, the Norwegian law thus significantly complicates the process of establishing whether a circumcision is legitimate, especially in comparison with the Swedish and German laws. The first complication is that it introduces a problematic norm, limiting which circumcisions are lawful, since non-medical circumcisions that are not religiously motivated appear to be excluded.

However, the purpose of the law, which is explicitly established under section 1, only states that it is 'to ensure that ritual circumcision of boys is carried out in a responsible manner, and that an offer of ritual circumcision is available', and thus does not mention that it intends to exclude certain non-religious forms.[8] This lack of acknowledgement that the law does restrict non-medical circumcision is especially interesting since the official proposal for the law (Prop. 70 L (2013–2014)) contained a section explaining its background, which opens with the following paragraph:

> Ritual circumcision of boys has been practised for thousands of years, and is today a common practice worldwide. It occurs within several population groups and is done for various reasons, including both religious, cultural and hygienic causes (Prop. 70 L (2013–2014) 2.1).[9]

Of the three reasons for ritual circumcision mentioned here – religious, cultural and hygienic – only the first is included under the current law. This might have been alleviated if 'religious' had been paired here with a secular equivalent, along the lines of 'belief'. Yet there is no provision for non-religious motivations being equally valid as religious ones, as occurs in other legal contexts discussed above.

While there is little data available on the reasons why parents choose to circumcise their children in European countries, individual stories show that people can be motivated by concerns that they themselves identify as non-religious yet highly

---

8 On the purpose of the law, see also Edler, Axelsson, Barker, Lie, Naumburg, 2016: 842.
9 'Rituell omskjæring av gutter har blitt praktisert i flere tusen år, og er i dag et vanlig inngrep stort sett over hele verden. Det forekommer innenfor flere befolkningsgrupper og gjøres av ulike årsaker, herunder både religiøse, kulturelle og hygieniske årsaker.'

significant. In an article in *The Atlantic*, Joshua Hammer, an American living in Berlin, describes how he sat down with his partner to discuss the circumcision of his son, who was about to be born. 'As an American Jew, I was adamant that Tom should be circumcised. Although I'm not religious, I pointed out that cutting off his foreskin would establish the Jewish part of his identity – an identity that I believed was important to declare in Germany' (Hammer, 2013). This example shows that parents can value circumcision for establishing an identity that has a particular historical significance, yet is explicitly not religious.

In a discussion on male circumcision in EU public hospitals, Margherita Brusa and Y. Michael Barilan (2009: 472) question the validity of the distinction between religious and cultural motivations: 'Even if "religion" and "culture" were independent entities, or maintained stable logical relationships with each other, we see no particular reason to find one context morally weightier than the other'. Brusa and Barilan suggest that gender and class may be factors in whether circumcision is presented as cultural or religious. They cite a survey in which Sudanese men interpreted female genital cutting as religious, whereas Sudanese women saw the same practice as 'a good tradition' (2009: 472).[10] The authors conclude that they 'do not see a reason for trying to rank the value of circumcision for Senegalese Christians relative to those of tribal Africans or observant Muslims. In the same vein, we do not suppose that the few religious sentiments of a secular person, even an atheist, deserve less consideration than the religious values of the most piously orthodox, or of one who follows the ways of an ethnic group without adherence to any creed whatsoever' (2009: 472).[11] This problem of ranking the value of circumcision is precisely the problem introduced with the requirement of religious motivations, and the possibility that the stated value differs according to regional, class and gender background, as these authors argue, can certainly not be excluded.

A further complication is, as we have seen, that religion tends to be equated with belief, and conceptions of religious freedom tend to protect religious ideas rather than actions. It is noteworthy then that while the law in this case intends to ensure a religious practice, rather than a belief, it requires that the purpose of the practice is religiously motivated. It thus assumes that motivations come before and determine the nature of actions and considers the individual and the cognitive to be decisive, in relation to a practice that can be experienced instead as collective and

---

10 Brusa and Barilan citing Gruenbaum, 2001: 49.
11 The authors conclude that male circumcision should be performed in the private, not the public health sector: 'Since cultural motivations are clearly unrelated to the medical treatment, and particularly since many healthcare professionals in Europe object to circumcision on moral grounds and even find it opposed to the very values of public and free healthcare, we propose that circumcision be performed by the private sector, and that consideration be given to public participation in the costs' (481).

constitutive, as the example of Joshua Hammer illustrates. It thereby reintroduces the bias criticised by Shakman Hurd, which normalises the idea that *believing* is taken as *the* universal defining characteristic of what it means to be religious, and excludes other modes of being or living religiously, for example, 'as bodies in communities to which they are obliged' (Hurd, 2012).

Finally, as we have seen, determining what is religious and what is not is both difficult and subjective. The lack of consensus about a definition of 'religion', and by implication of 'religious', and the inherent Protestant bias prevalent in many views may prove problematic in assessing the legitimacy of any circumcision. Two recent rulings on male circumcision from Germany, in which such Protestant understandings of religion can be seen to play a role, can give some idea of the assumptions that inform legal opinions on circumcision in the European context that has been shaped by Christianity.

3. Circumcision, religion and law: two German cases

3.1 Circumcision and the freedom of religion

The first of the rulings to be discussed here dates from the spring of 2012, when the Cologne Regional Court decided on the case of a doctor who circumcised a four-year old Muslim boy, at the request of his parents.[12] While most court cases that deal with circumcision are the result of a disagreement between parents, this case had a more complicated origin. Shortly after his circumcision, the boy in question was taken to the emergency department of a hospital due to complications. There it was assumed that the circumcision had not been performed according to medical standards, and the authorities were brought in, which eventually led to a charge against the physician who had performed the circumcision.[13] He was accused of causing bodily harm to another person by using a dangerous instrument, but was acquitted, first by the Cologne Local Court and after a subsequent appeal, by the Regional Court. The grounds given for the acquittal were that the doctor was convinced that his actions were lawful, and that this mistake was unavoidable, since 'the question whether a circumcision for religious reasons at the request of the parents is lawful is not answered uniformly in the case law and literature' (Orth, 2013: 505).

---

12 Landgericht Köln, 151 Ns 169/11 (07–05–2012). For the court's findings, see http://dejure.org/dienste/vernetzung/rechtsprechung?Gericht=LG%20K%F6ln&Datum=07.05.2012&Aktenzeichen=151%20Ns%20169/11.

13 For details of the case and the verdict, see Orth, 2013: 497–511.

The Cologne Regional Court, however, did consider religiously motivated male circumcision to be a form of bodily harm and even in some sense 'a criminal assault', and therefore a violation of the boy's rights (Orth, 2013: 502). In addition to weighing arguments about the bodily integrity and autonomy of the child, the court also discussed arguments related to religion, notably the religious freedom of the parents, as well the presumed effects that circumcision would have on the boy's freedom of religion.

Given the international interest in the case, the court's decision was explained for an English-language audience by the court spokesperson for this case, Jan F. Orth, in an article in *The Journal of Criminal Law*. Orth here rejects the notion that this decision is discriminatory in nature, as has been claimed. He rather believes that it shows a 'remarkably liberal approach, although references from its holding may indeed limit religious communities in practising circumcisions' (Orth, 2013: 497). He further denies the suggestion that the court did not take the freedom of religion of the parents into sufficient account. According to Orth, the verdict shows that 'religious interests and rights have been regarded. The court's weighing up of them simply ended in favour of the individual rights of the child. This is the core of the decision.' (2013: 503) Orth cites the court's finding in this respect as follows:

> The principle of proportionality must be taken into account when striking the balance between these rights. The infringement of bodily integrity caused by a circumcision for purposes of religious education is unreasonable in the sense of proportionality, even if necessary to that end … [T]he circumcision changes the child's body permanently and irreparably. This change runs contrary to the interests of the child in deciding his religious affiliation independently later in life. On the other hand, the parental right of education is not unacceptably diminished by requiring them to wait until their son is able to make the decision himself whether to have a circumcision as a visible sign of his affiliation to Islam … (Orth, 2013: 503).[14]

The verdict thus understands religion to be primarily a matter not of the child, but of the adult that he will become. The interest of the boy is to be able to 'decide' his religious affiliation 'later in life'.[15] Circumcision is then assumed to cause a

---

14 The German text of this section of the verdict is 'Zudem wird der Körper des Kindes durch die Beschneidung dauerhaft und irreparabel verändert. Diese Veränderung läuft dem Interesse des Kindes später selbst über seine Religionszugehörigkeit entscheiden zu können zuwider. Umgekehrt wird das Erziehungsrecht der Eltern nicht unzumutbar beeinträchtigt, wenn sie gehalten sind abzuwarten, ob sich der Knabe später, wenn er mündig ist, selbst für die Beschneidung als sichtbares Zeichen der Zugehörigkeit zum Islam entscheidet.'
15 For an earlier analysis on the understanding of both religion and gender that inform this verdict and subsequent legal discourse, see Neutel, 2021.

permanent change to the boy's body that will impair his ability to freely make this religious decision. Although it is not made explicit, the reasoning of the court appears to be that a circumcised boy is already bound to a certain religious tradition by the physical 'change' that he has undergone, which is therefore considered to be a violation of his religious freedom. How the body impacts religion and why the physical change of the boy limits the religious freedom of the man is not explained, but taken as a given.

These various assumptions all appear to rest on an understanding of religion that is familiar from the discussion of legal definitions above, as well as from the 'Protestant' templates for religion, which form the starting point for this volume. Religion is a matter for the individual, something that should be decided on freely, and without undue influence, including that of parents. There appears to be no awareness here of the bias associated with a Christian, belief-centred, understanding of religion, which inevitably sees a bodily practice such as circumcision as secondary.

After brief but heated political and cultural debate in Germany, the Bundestag adopted a new law on male circumcision, in December 2012. This law explicitly legalizes circumcision of boys for non-medical reasons when performed according to medical standards. As discussed at the beginning of this article, this law does not mention any motivations as a requirement, religious, or otherwise.

3.2 Circumcision, masculinity and baptism

Yet religion can be an important factor, and even criterion, when the law is applied in a German court, as is evident in an August 2013 verdict by the Oberlandesgericht Hamm.[16] This case involved a dispute between a mother who wanted to have her then six-year-old son, identified as 'G', circumcised, and the father, from whom she had been divorced, who wanted to prevent the circumcision. The Court of Appeal upheld the initial verdict, which decided against allowing the mother to go through with the circumcision since this was seen as potentially harmful for the child.

The verdict starts out by acknowledging that the 2012 law 'in principle' grants parents the right to decide to circumcise minor children without medical indication, based on 'autonomous cultural-ritual reasons' ('aus autonomen kulturellrituellen Gründen'). Such reasons are not specified in the text of the law, nor are they further clarified in this verdict. In a subsequent more detailed section of the verdict (II 2.a), it is granted that parents – in this case the mother who had sole custody – have the right to circumcise regardless of their motivations ('ohne dass es auf die Motivation der Eltern ankommt').

---

16 Oberlandesgericht Hamm, Beschl. v. 30.08.2013, Az.: 3 UF 133/13. See https://openjur.de/u/646212.html.

The ruling nevertheless goes on to examine the reasons that the mother has put forward for wanting the boy's circumcision. The first of these is that circumcision is in accordance with the cultural custom of Kenya ('in Kenia kulturell üblichen Ritus'), which is where she and much of the boy's family were from. On visits there, he would otherwise not be seen as a full man. This, it is stated, is the rule for all boys in Africa ('In Afrika sei das so, alle Jungen müssten das machen'). His relatives therefore ask in every phone call whether G has been circumcised yet. The second reason given for the circumcision is connected to hygiene and cleanliness.

In its evaluation, the verdict acknowledges that both motives can justify a non-medical circumcision. It goes on to object, however, that since the mother and her son have their home in Germany, where the mother has remarried, and the boy has his school and friends, they are in fact rarely able to visit Kenya. It is further stated that G has 'indisputably undergone Protestant baptism, and therefore religious grounds do not indicate circumcision', a point to which we will return below. Reasons of hygiene are rejected by the court as insufficient, on the grounds that the mother has not put forward any specific concerns about dangerous conditions which would result from not circumcising him. The verdict rather expects the boy to achieve the appropriate levels of intimate hygiene, just like the majority of German children, who are not circumcised.

It is further counted against the wish to circumcise that the practice is self-evident, or, as the court puts it 'a must', from the Kenyan cultural perspective of the mother. The verdict notes a lack of 'critical reflection' about possible implications for the welfare of the child ('Im Übrigen lassen die Motive, soweit sie wegen des kenianischen kulturellen Erfordernisses von einem "Muss" der Beschneidung ausgehen, kaum eine kritische Reflexion der Kindesmutter über die Folgen für das Kindeswohl erkennen'). The familiarity of the mother with the practice thus appears to conflict with the court's expectation of how the decision to circumcise should be reached. Concerns raised by the father and by several professionals involved with the child, including a psychologist, that G's wellbeing is threatened by the circumcision, are ultimately seen to outweigh the mother's motivations.

Interesting for our focus here is the role of religion, which is not mentioned as part of the reasons for circumcision, but rather counts against its validity for the court. The verdict raises the boy's church affiliation as part of the evaluation of the mother's arguments, yet this is not directly related to her stated reasons for circumcision, which have to do with masculinity and hygiene. Yet it is somehow seen as relevant that G has 'indisputably' undergone Protestant baptism, and that as a presumed consequence of this 'religious grounds do not indicate circumcision' ('Zudem ist G unstreitig evangelisch getauft, sodass religiöse Gründe keine Beschneidung anzeigen'). In a quite narrow Protestant European view – which is by no means shared by Protestants the world over – baptism and circumcision are presented here as mutually exclusive religious rites.[17]

The fact that the verdict explicitly argues that religious motivations are absent here, albeit on shaky grounds that clearly betray a Eurocentric Christian perspective, suggests that such religious motives would have constituted important arguments for the court, if they had been included. The absence of religious motivations is then taken as an indication of the relative weight of what is put forward instead.

The verdict in this case is thus informative for our exploration in that it shows that even when there is no requirement to give religious motivations for circumcision, such as there is under Norwegian law, religion still presents the implicit and Christocentric norm for what counts as important in legitimating a parent's wish to circumcise.

4. Concluding thoughts

By stipulating religious motivations as a requirement for legitimate non-medical circumcision, the Norwegian law introduces several complications. Religion is a contested and loosely defined concept, which makes it difficult to achieve a valid distinction between religious and non-religious motivations. Moreover, as Brusa and Barilan suggest, there might well be gender, class, educational and other social biases involved in argumentations for circumcision, which would make the expressions of some groups more acceptable than those of others, regardless of individual motivations. In addition, privileging religion over non-religion runs counter to an important recent tendency to challenge the position of religion as deserving of special protection. By requiring religious motivations, the law not only reinstates religion as of crucial importance, but also makes motivations the key factor that legitimates circumcision. It thereby reflects the Protestant view that internal belief is the essence of religion and that any religious practice is only a secondary manifestation of internal conviction, not a constitutive part of religion itself. Yet as the German cases discussed here show, not specifying religious motivation does not guarantee the absence of religion as a norm either. The Protestant understanding of religion appears to be so closely tied up with majority views on circumcision

---

17 Exact numbers are difficult to determine for circumcision, but the World Health Organisation estimates that approximately 30% of the world's males aged 15 years or older are circumcised. This is over 660 million men, of whom 200 million are counted by the WHO as 'non-religious' (meaning neither Jewish nor Muslim) circumcisions. In some countries where the population is predominantly Christian, and presumably baptised, such as the US, the Philippines, and Kenya, circumcision rates can be as high as 75–90% (World Health Organisation, 'Male circumcision: global trends and determinants of prevalence, safety and acceptability' 2007).

that the practice can hardly be evaluated apart from it, even, or especially, in a legal context.

Bibliography

Aldridge, Alan. *Religion in the Contemporary World – A Sociological Introduction* (3rd edition, Cambridge: Polity Press, 2013).
Brusa, Margherita and Y. Michael Barilan. 'Cultural Circumcision in EU Public Hospitals: An Ethical Discussion' *Bioethics* 23/8 (2009): 470–482.
Dressler, Markus and Arvind Mandair (eds.). *Secularism and Religion-Making* (Oxford: Oxford University Press, 2011).
Dubuisson, Daniel. *The Western Construction of Religion: Myths, Knowledge, and Ideology* (Baltimore: The Johns Hopkins University Press 2003).
Edler, Gertrud, Inge Axelsson, Gillian M. Barker, Susanne Lie, Estelle Naumburg. 'Serious Complications in Male Infant Circumcisions in Scandinavia Indicate that this Always Be Performed as a Hospital-based Procedure'. *Acta Pædiatrica* 105/7 (2016): 842–850.
Erlings, Esther I.J. 'The Law and Practices of Ritual Male Circumcision: Time for Review'. In: Sibnath Deb (ed.), *Child Safety, Welfare and Well-being: Issues and Challenges* (New Delhi: Springer, 2016), 95–113.
European Commission, Directorate-General for Employment, Social Affairs and Inclusion, Lucy Vickers. *Religion and belief discrimination in employment: the EU law*, Publications Office, 2007.
Feldman, Stephen M. (ed.). *Law and Religion: A Critical Anthology* (New York: New York University, 2000), 262–266.
Gruenbaum, Ellen. *The Female Circumcision Controversy: An Anthropological Perspective* (Philadelphia: University of Pennsylvania Press, 2001), 49.
Gunn, T. Jeremy. 'The Complexity of Religion and the Definition of "Religion" in International Law'. *Harvard Human Rights Journal* 16 (2003): 189–215.
Hammer, Joshua. 'Anti-Semitism and Germany's Movement Against Circumcision'. *The Atlantic* January 7, 2013.
Hurd, Elizabeth Shakman. 'Believing in religious freedom'. *The Immanent Frame*, March 1, 2012.
Idinopulos, Thomas A. and Brian Courtney Wilson (eds.). *What is Religion? Origins, Definitions and Explanations* (Leiden: Brill, 1998).
Jakobsen, Janet R. 'Religion'. In: Bruce Burgett and Glenn Hendler (eds.). *Keywords for American Cultural Studies* (New York: NYU Press 2014^2), 215–217.
King, Richard. 'Imagining Religions in India: Colonialism and the Mapping of South Asian History and Culture'. In: Markus Dressler and Arvind Mandair (eds.), *Secularism and Religion-Making* (Oxford: Oxford University Press, 2011): 37–61.

Laborde, Cécile. 'Three approaches to the study of religion'. *The Immanent Frame* February 5, 2014, https://tif.ssrc.org/2014/02/05/three-approaches-to-the-study-of-religion/.

Landgericht Köln, 151 Ns 169/11 (07–05–2012). For the court's findings, see http://dejure.org/dienste/vernetzung/rechtsprechung?Gericht=LG%20K%F6ln&Datum=07.05.2012&Aktenzeichen=151%20Ns%20169/11 (last accessed Aug. 2022).

Lindkvist, Linde. 'The Politics of Article 18: Religious Liberty in the Universal Declaration of Human Rights'. *Humanity: An International Journal of Human Rights, Humanitarianism, and Development* 4 (2013): 429–447.

Masuzawa, Tomoko. *The Invention of World Religions: Or, How European Universalism was Preserved in the Language of Pluralism* (Chicago: The University of Chicago Press, 2005).

Neutel, Karin. 'Shedding Religious Skin: An Intersectional Analysis of the Claim that Male Circumcision Limits Religious Freedom'. In: Valérie Nicolet Anderson and Marianne Bjelland Kartzow (eds.), *The Complexity of Conversion: Intersectional Perspectives on Religious Change in Antiquity and Beyond* (Sheffield: Equinox, 2021).

Nongbri, Brent. *Before Religion: A History of a Modern Concept* (New Haven: Yale University Press, 2013).

Nurser, John. 'The "Ecumenical Movement", Churches, "Global Order" and Human Rights: 1938-1948'. *Human Rights Quarterly* 25 (2003): 841–881.

Orth, Jan F. 'Explaining the Cologne Circumcision Decision'. *The Journal of Criminal Law* 77/6 (2013), 497–511.

Platvoet, Jan G. and Arie L. Molendijk (eds.). *The Pragmatics of Defining Religion: Contexts, Concepts and Contests* (Leiden: Brill, 1999).

Sullivan, Winnifred F. *The Impossibility of Religious Freedom* (Princeton: Princeton University Press, 2005).

Sandberg, Russell. *Religion, Law and Society* (Cambridge: Cambridge University Press, 2014).

Sandberg, Russell. 'Clarifying the Definition of Religion Under English Law: The Need for a Universal Definition'. *Ecclesiastical Law Journal* 20/2 (2018), 132–157.

Sherwood, Yvonne. 'On the Freedom of the Concepts of Religion and Belief'. In: W. F. Sullivan et al. (eds.). *Politics of Religious Freedom* (Chicago: Chicago University Press, 2015), 29–44.

Swatek-Evenstein, Mark. 'Limits of Enlightenment and the Law: On the Legality of Ritual Male Circumcision in Europe Today'. *Merkourios* 29/77 (2013): 42–50.

Schiratzki, Johanna. 'Banning God's Law in the Name of The Holy Body: The Nordic Position on Ritual Male Circumcision'. *The Family in Law* 5 (2011): 35–53.

Tambiah, Stanley J. *Magic, Science and Religion and the Scope of Rationality* (Cambridge: Cambridge University Press, 1990).

Woodhead, Linda. 'Five Concepts of Religion'. *International Review of Sociology* 21.1 (2011): 121–143.

World Health Organization, Department of Reproductive Health and Research and Joint United Nations Programme on HIV/AIDS (UNAIDS). *Male circumcision: global trends and determinants of prevalence, safety and acceptability* (2007). Available from: http://whqlibdoc.who.int/publications/2007/9789241596169_eng.pdf?ua=1

Laws and rulings

Lag om omskärelse av pojkar (2001:499). https://www.riksdagen.se/sv/dokument-lagar/dokument/svensk-forfattningssamling/lag-2001499-om-omskarelse-av-pojkar_sfs-2001-499

Lov om rituell omskjæring av gutter. Lov om rituell omskjæring av gutter av 20. juni 2014 nr.40. https://lovdata.no/dokument/NL/lov/2014-06-20-40

Bürgerliches Gesetzbuch, Abschnitt 2 – Verwandtschaft, § 1631d Beschneidung des männlichen Kindes https://dejure.org/gesetze/BGB/1631d.html (last accessed Aug. 2022).

Oberlandesgericht Hamm, Beschl. v. 30.08.2013, Az.: 3 UF 133/13. See https://openjur.de/u/646212.html (last accessed Aug. 2022).

Vebjørn L. Horsfjord

Chapter 5: Protestantisations in the Norwegian Debate on Circumcision

Introduction

Ritual male circumcision is on the agenda as an object for potential state regulation or prohibition in many European countries, not least in those countries in the north of Europe where the Protestant tradition has been or remains strong. This chapter will explore some of the complex relationships between the Protestant heritage and attitudes to circumcision.[1] Although it is at best hard to establish a causal relationship between a culture marked by the Protestant tradition and critical views on circumcision, it is possible to point out certain correlations between understandings of religion that we may call typically Protestant and a readiness to regulate circumcision as performed by the Muslim and Jewish minorities in traditionally Protestant countries. Based on analyses of a body of texts from Norwegian newspapers, I ask how Protestant formatting of religion finds expression in the debate on ritual male circumcision and how the phenomenon of "protestantisation" is brought explicitly into the debate.

After a brief introduction to the circumcision debate in Norway and the material under study, I will introduce a claim, found within the material, that opposition to circumcision is guided by a "Lutheran mindset". This leads to a discussion on three closely related notions: that the "inner" is more important than the "outward" when it comes to religion, that religion ought to be freely chosen, and that religion should be able to develop progressively and leave tradition behind. A fourth version of protestantisation is represented in the claim that Protestant formatting of religion leads observers to privilege normative and scriptural traditions over lived religion.

---

1 In this chapter I will sometimes use the term "circumcision" as shorthand for "ritual male circumcision" or "ritual circumcision of baby boys and young boys" when the meaning is clear from the context. Terminology on this topic is a minefield where the choice of words sometimes signals specific positions. Difficulties especially arise when the removal of the foreskin of the penis of young boys is compared to removal of parts of the genitals of young girls. Those who see these as closely related often prefer to call them by the same name, either by using the term "circumcision" also when female genitals are involved, or insisting that male circumcision is "genital mutilation", a term most often reserved for practices pertaining to girls. The term "cutting" and derivatives can also arouse strong emotions. Although the choice of words is prone to elicit objections from one camp or the other, a choice has to be made.

This claim is proffered in the debate *against* circumcision. Based on the findings, I will conclude with a discussion on the usefulness of the notion of protestantisation.

Background

In June 2014 the Norwegian parliament passed into law an Act that for the first time regulates the practice of male ritual circumcision. The new legislation, which came into force in January 2015, stipulates that male circumcision can only be performed by or under the supervision of a medical doctor, and requires the public health service to provide circumcision to parents who request it, either by offering it in public hospitals or by contracting it to private clinics. Those who request circumcision for their children must pay a fee, but this does not fully cover the costs involved.

The Act was introduced with the intention of regulating the practice and ensuring the medical quality of circumcisions while at the same time not curbing the Jewish practice of Brit Mila. In the White Paper preceding the new legislation the Ministry of Health and Care Services estimated that around 2000 boys underwent circumcision each year in Norway, of whom less than ten were Jews and the rest were Muslims (Ministry of Health and Care Services, 2011: 13).

The new legislation was first proposed in 2011, and relevant organisations, including faith communities as well as those representing various medical professions, were invited to comment on the proposal. This sparked a public debate that has tended to focus less on the details of the proposed legislation and more on whether or not to ban circumcision or to introduce an age limit, usually set at 15 or 16. No ban or age limit has ever been proposed by the government.

For various reasons the proposal was put on hold, and after the first round of debates in 2011, public discussions ebbed until around September 2013 when the Ombudspersons for Children in the Nordic countries issued a joint statement in which they argued for banning circumcision on those under the age of 15 or 16. The Norwegian ombudsperson at the time, who is also a paediatrician, appears to have taken the lead on this issue. Around the same time, it became clear that the newly elected government would introduce what later became the new Act to parliament. Thus the issue was intensely debated throughout the rest of 2013 and until the Act was passed by parliament in June 2014. In the spring of 2017, the issue once again became a hot news item when a possible age limit on male circumcision was debated by several political parties at their annual conferences in preparation for the general election in September 2017. One party, the Progress Party, which was part of the governing alliance, made a ban on circumcision their official position.

In this chapter I will draw on quantitative and qualitative analyses of newspaper texts on male circumcision in the print editions of 12 significant Norwegian newspapers from 1 July 2013 (one year before the new legislation was passed by Parliament) until 30 June 2017 (at the end of the party conference season).[2] The material consists of 436 texts that have been analysed and coded for, *inter alia*, their origin, date, genre, author, main attitude to circumcision (critical, neutral or positive), their framing of circumcision (is it about health, religious freedom, Jews, Muslims, anti-Semitism etc.) and the topics mentioned (from a list similar to that of the framing issues).[3] Sections of the texts were further coded for a range of relevant topics, such as "secularisation", "health", "children's right to choose", "protestantisation", "female genital mutilation" and so on.[4]

The law and religion

The public debate on circumcision, which undoubtedly was sparked by the proposal (and later implementation) of legislation to regulate the practice, to a very limited extent concerned concrete aspects of the law. On the contrary, contributors to the debate tend to argue for or against circumcision (or the imposing of an age limit) although no ban or age limit was part of the proposal. However, the law on male circumcision in its very structure raises questions about the various ways of formatting religion. Even the title draws attention to circumcision as a religious practice: "Act relating to *ritual* circumcision" [emphasis added], and the first paragraph of the Act specifies that its purpose is "to ensure that *ritual circumcision* of boys is performed in a responsible manner" [emphasis added].[5] Section two provides a definition of ritual circumcision and reads *in extentio*: "In this Act, ritual circumcision means

---

2 The selection of newspapers is based on circulation figures. The 12 newspapers are, in alphabetical order Adresseavisen, Aftenposten, Bergens Tidende, Dagbladet, Dagen, Dagsavisen, Klassekampen, Morgenbladet (weekly), Nationen, Stavanger Aftenblad, VG and Vårt Land.
3 The material was harvested from the Retriever/Atekst database. A total of 1380 texts from the period contained the Norwegian word for circumcision/circumcise or derivatives ("omskjær*", "omskjer*" etc.). The majority of these dealt only with female circumcision and were excluded from further analysis. 144 of the remaining 580 texts were further excluded because they either dealt with male circumcision without reference to Norway, or touched on the matter in passing without adding any substance to the debate (for example by listing circumcision among agenda items at a party conference). The remaining 436 newspaper texts form the material that has been analysed further.
4 The qualitative part of the analysis was conducted with the help of Nvivo software which allows for easy retrieval of sections of texts coded to the same topic, and also allows for combining qualitative and quantitative coding. A more quantitatively oriented analysis of the same material, focused on how various actors frame the topic of male circumcision, can be found in Horsfjord (2020).
5 There is no official English version of the Act. Translations of the Act here are my own.

surgery whereby the foreskin of the penis is partially or fully removed and where the purpose is religious".[6] In other words, the Act assumes that "ritual circumcision" is performed for religious reasons, and expressly states that it does not regulate circumcision that is not motivated by religion. Circumcision for medical reasons will obviously continue to be performed and falls under general legislation pertaining to medical treatment, but if parents want to have a boy circumcised for non-medical reasons without giving a religious reason, that would not be allowed. This is not a common scenario in Norway, but many participants in the debate regularly point to the US, where male circumcision is widespread without an explicit religious basis.

This has at least two interesting implications: First, those who perform circumcisions on behalf of the state can in principle find themselves in situations where they have to evaluate the reasons for a concrete request for circumcision and decide whether it is religious enough to fulfil the requirements in the Act. There are no traces of such challenges in the material under investigation. Secondly, however, the Act implicitly insists on a religious versus non-religious dichotomy that runs counter to some of the arguments in favour of circumcision. I will return to this presently.

The term "protestantisation" does not occur in the material under investigation.[7] In fact, there is no trace of it ever having been used in printed mainstream media in Norway.[8] Indeed, the term "Protestant" (or derivatives) occurs very infrequently, and in only two of the texts in the material is it used in such a way that it sheds light on the contribution of the influence of the Protestant heritage on the debate.[9] "Protestantisation", "Protestant" and "Protestantism" in this analysis are therefore primarily analytical terms that are applied from an outsider perspective on those involved in the debate. As in many other chapters in this volume, the notion of protestantisation is inspired by Peter Berger's use (Berger, 2007). Some of the characteristics of ideal Protestantism are that it is freely chosen, held with a strong conviction and privileges "inner faith" over "outward ritual" (ibid.). Protestantisation, then, is a process whereby other religious traditions are measured against such ideals, expected to conform to them or gradually adopt features associated with ideal Protestantism.

---

6 Norwegian: "…og hvor formålet er religiøst begrunnet".
7 Norwegian: "protestantisering".
8 The term does not occur anywhere in the extremely extensive material covered by the media database Retriever/Atekst.
9 An overview (in Norwegian) of how "Protestant" and "Protestantism" are used as a cliché in contemporary Norwegian newspaper texts is found in Horsfjord (2017).

Jewish criticism of "a Lutheran perspective"

Although "Protestantism" and "protestantisation" primarily function as analytical tools that can yield insights into the formation and formatting of the understanding of religion in and through discussions on circumcision, some of the insights that they convey are occasionally expressed by those who participate in the debate. The clearest example is in a text by Ervin Kohn, the president of the Jewish community in Oslo and one of the most prominent contributors to the public debate on male circumcision.[10] Responding to an article that called for more space for religious arguments in the circumcision debate and observed that by using medical arguments in favour of circumcision Kohn tended to "accept the hegemony of secular arguments", Kohn said:

> These attitudes are commendable. However, [their] frame of reference is Lutheran, and within these frames religion is spirituality. For this reason it is not uncommon to speak about the degree to which one believes…To ask a Jew, or for that matter a Muslim, the degree to which he believes will often lead to uncertainty rather than a clear answer. But if you ask the Jew about the degree to which s/he practices, the answer will come more promptly…The Jewish religion is a mix of philosophy and rules for daily life (Kohn, 2013).[11]

Kohn then goes on to problematize the distinction between religious and secular arguments. He explains that the commandment to circumcise baby boys on their eighth day (Brit Mila) is found in the Torah, but claims that it would not have been practised so widely by Jews if they were not convinced that it had positive effects on their children's health: "I am convinced that the requirement to perform Brit Mila has been given to us because there are health benefits, not because the disadvantages are minimal" (ibid.).

Kohn's claim about a Lutheran frame of reference amounts to an analysis very similar to what we otherwise call "protestantisation". Within such a frame of reference, the core of religion is inner "spirituality" rather than outward material expression. A "religious argument", he seems to suggest, is an argument that follows from a sincerely held inner conviction, which – as religious – is not necessarily shared by those of other religions or none at all. Against this, he posits the claim that at the centre of "the Jewish religion" are rules for daily life, or "outward expressions" in Protestant terminology. However, it does not logically follow that religious "rules for daily life" do not require religious arguments. As the extracts from the texts

---

10 Kohn's name is mentioned in 85 of the 436 texts in the material.
11 This and subsequent translations from Norwegian newspaper texts are my own.

make clear, Kohn further insists that these daily life rules, or at least the rule to circumcise baby boys, are reasonable beyond the inner logic of a religious tradition: It has health benefits which can be discussed and recognised without reference to any religious tradition. Kohn consequently fights on two fronts: Against those who seek to limit the right to circumcision (even when this is unreasonable from a health perspective) and also against those who defend his right, but in the same operation impose a Protestant frame of mind on him.

Kohn, however, does not only challenge a Protestant formatting of his "Jewish religion", but brings the dichotomy between the religious and the non-religious into play. An obvious question arising from his argument would be: What would you do if you became convinced that circumcision does not have positive health implications? Merely the absence of disadvantages, it seems, would not compel him to follow the commandments laid down in the Torah. Taken to its logical conclusion, Kohn's argument does not allow him to seek refuge from medical counter arguments, neither in an appeal to respect for religious arguments nor in religious freedom. This, however, also in principle presents him with problems when it comes to the Act that was explicitly designed to protect his right to Brit Mila.[12] As I pointed out above, the Act only regulates circumcisions that are "based on religion", that is, some form of religious argument seems to be a requirement for a non-medical circumcision to be in accordance with the Act. Convictions that circumcision offers health benefits alone are not enough to make circumcision legal, unless the reasons in an individual case are strong enough to support a medical intervention, in which case it would fall under general medical legislation and not that specifically regulating circumcision. Without the dichotomy between the religious and the non-religious, the Act would lose its field of application and thus collapse.

This latter point is similar to, but not identical with, the challenge that arises for religious freedom arguments in favour of circumcision if reference to religious tradition becomes an optional part of the argument. Although the Act does not specifically mention religious freedom, it is clear that part of its rationale is to protect the religious freedom of Muslims and Jews. As pointed out elsewhere in this volume, implementation of the right to freedom of religion requires a distinction between that which is religious (and therefore protected) and that which is not, and also a constant negotiation of where the boundary between the two is found. Again, a conviction about health benefits on its own does not constitute a religious

---

12 The Act's provision that circumcisions do not have to be performed by a medical doctor, only that they must be done under a medical doctor's supervision, is clearly designed to allow the Jewish practice in which a trained circumciser, *mohel*, performs the actual circumcision. The requirement to have a medical doctor present does not infringe on the traditional Jewish ritual. Muslims are generally happy to let medical doctors circumcise their young boys.

conviction and consequently does not merit protection under freedom of religion rules.

Kohn's argument, therefore, if taken not merely as strategic positioning vis-à-vis a hegemonic medical discourse, might undermine his primary aim, to secure the possibility to perform Brit Mila. This, however, does not necessarily expose a flaw in his argument, but rather the strength of the Protestant formatting – or in Kohn's own words, the "Lutheran frame of mind" – that is implied by the new Act. It is an irony that an Act that is explicitly designed to protect religious minorities may presuppose an understanding of religion that is foreign to the same minorities. Legal protection, it seems, is also a forced protestantisation of the Jewish tradition, and if Jews resist protestantisation by escaping the religious–non-religious dichotomy, they also lose the legal protection.

Outward expression and inward reality – sign and signified

Kohn's claim that Lutheranism frames religion as spirituality is very similar to the claim that Protestantism tends to privilege the inner over the outer. A sharp inward–outward distinction with a privileging of the inward is a central feature of a Protestant formatting of religion. We may understand this as related to the widely held Protestant conviction that inner "faith" matters more than outward "works", but we should also see it in light of an understanding of the relationship between sign and signified that is widespread in the Protestant tradition. We find a typical example in a comment from a member of parliament for the Norwegian Labour Party, who favours a 15year age limit, and says that "I think both Jews and Muslims are open to discuss…*what circumcision really means*" [emphasis added] (Våge, 2014). Another representative example of the privileging of inner convictions over outward "signs" or "expressions" is found in the Ombudsperson for Children's official comments on the first White Paper in 2011 when she "encourages adults in the different faith communities" to find alternative ways to "help children to express their religious belonging" (Norwegian Ombudsperson for Children, 2011: 8). The underlying assumption in such statements is that there is a primary, inner reality (belonging or faith) that seeks external expression, and that this expression in principle is arbitrary. The Ombudsperson further underlines the possibility to change the expression (or sign) without changing the inner reality of belonging when in this specific context it is pointed out that one is aware that "within Judaism there are believers ["troende"] who practise Brit Shalom which is a name-giving ceremony and an alternative to circumcision" (ibid.).[13]

---

13 The argument in the Ombudsperson's original document is supported by a reference to Wikipedia.

Having alternative rituals to circumcision is a recurring topic in texts in the material that argue for a ban or age limit. By insisting on a weak or arbitrary relationship between sign and signified, one can insist that there is space for choice within the religious sphere. When this is established, the assumption is that society can also require parents to make a specific choice in favour of a sign that does not leave a mark on the child's body.

Within the Protestant tradition the relationship between the outward sign and the "reality" it signifies has been most explicitly thought through with regard to one of the most central Christian rituals, the Eucharist. Established Catholic and Orthodox theology emphasises the "real presence" of Christ in the bread and wine consumed as part of the ritual and consequently attaches great significance to details of how the ritual is performed, the quality of the consumed elements and how unconsumed bread and wine are to be treated after the ritual. On the other side of the scale, within the Reformed tradition, as well as the more radical branches of the Protestant tradition (Baptism and Pentecostalism), the ritual consumption of bread and wine is understood to *remind* participants of Christ, but a clear distinction is upheld between the sign (bread and wine) and the signified (Christ).

As is the case with many theological issues, the official Lutheran position is somewhere between the Catholic and the Reformed positions. However, it is safe to assume that popular understanding of the Eucharist among ordinary Lutherans in Norway in practice is closer to the Reformed than the Catholic position. Bearing this in mind, it is not surprising that the notion that the sign (circumcision) *is* in fact what it signifies (belonging, Jewishness) seems foreign to many in the Norwegian context.

A gap in perception between official Lutheran theology and popular understanding of Protestantism that leans more towards the Reformed tradition may explain an apparent paradox regarding protestantised lines of argument in the circumcision debate: The type of protestantised arguments that I have explored so far are consistently *not* found among those who officially represent the Lutheran church. When such representatives speak on the issue, they are without exception positively inclined towards circumcision, and they repeatedly underline the intimate and non-arbitrary connection between Jewish belonging and circumcision. Rather than in church circles, the most protestantised lines of argument thrive among those inclined towards secularism.

Freely chosen and deeply held

The importance of choice operates on two levels within arguments in favour of a ban or age limit on circumcision. The distinction between sign and signified, outward "expression" and inward "faith", provides space to choose how to express religious belief or belonging once such belonging is a reality. However, the freedom to choose whether to belong (or believe) is perhaps even more important. The expectation that religious belonging ideally should be the result of a free and informed choice belongs to the core of a Protestant formatting of religion (Berger, 2007: 19). The topic of children's right to choose religion is touched upon in more than four in ten of all the texts under investigation (188 out of the 436), and 122 of these make it the key question that decides the attitude to circumcision. Framing the question as one pertaining to free choice overwhelmingly coincides with a critical attitude towards circumcision, and only 12 of the 122 texts display a positive attitude. "Consent" is a key term in this context.[14] The term itself appears in about 16 per cent of all texts.

The discussion on consent can be seen in light of the theology surrounding another important Christian ritual, that of baptism. Some of those who oppose a ban seek to counter arguments about the need for consent by pointing to the practice of baptising children with the implicit or explicit claim that an age limit on circumcision based on the need for consent should also require an age limit on baptism (which is assumed to be absurd) (Rønsen, 2017). However, although the *ad absurdum* argument appears logical, these critics overlook that precisely the question about baptism of children has been at the core of intra-Christian discussions. Among Baptists and, later, among Pentecostal Christians, the notion that baptism, and therefore the highest level of belonging or identification with the community of believers, requires a free choice (consent), has been a defining feature. In fact, Berger's model Protestantism is Pentecostalism of which a central characteristic is the rejection of children's baptism (Berger, 2007:19–20).

Requiring consent is not the same as insisting that the sign (circumcision or baptism) is arbitrary. In this regard the Baptist Christian tradition does not provide support for the Ombudsperson for children's idea that one ritual (Brit Shalom) can easily substitute for another (Brit Mila). Full immersion in water is generally regarded as the only valid baptism. There is no arbitrariness about the sign, or rather, baptism is "the real thing" itself in the same way as circumcision itself is "the real thing" for many Jews. However, in the youngest branch of the broader Baptist tradition, Pentecostalism, there is a tendency to emphasise "baptism in the spirit" more than "baptism in water", underlining that the former neither coincides with nor depends on the latter. Baptism in the spirit, although considered "real", does not take a specific material form and may thus find a variety of concrete expressions. This position is only a step away from the fully secularised position of the Ombudsperson for children that that the real thing – freely chosen belonging or inner conviction – can find expression through an arbitrary outward sign.

---

14 Norwegian "samtykke".

Narratives of breaks and progress, or continuity with the past

The significance of time plays a role in the public discussion on male circumcision on both sides of the debate. The fact that Muslims and, especially, Jews have "always" practised circumcision is counted in its favour by those who argue against a ban or age limit, even if they are careful to underline that the old age of a practice in itself is not an argument in favour of its continuation (corporeal punishment is cited as an example of this on both sides). The appeal to circumcision's long history is combined with warnings against the idea that "our time" is in a uniquely privileged position to evaluate the past:

> The main premise [among those who argue in favour of a ban] is the assumption that Norway has reached a level of enlightenment and development that enables us to evaluate the world's cultures and religions in a neutral and impartial way. One aspect of this is a strong and naïve faith in science, especially medical science (Brekke, 2013).

According to another pundit, circumcision is "the answer to a command that chimes through millennia, a covenant that unites Jews across the ages" (Nyhus, 2017). Circumcision's long roots are used not least to counter "what if" arguments that imagine practices that could be invented today and given a religious foundation, for example cutting an earlobe. Those who use the long-roots argument maintain that traditions that have a long pedigree should be considered in a different light than new ideas that might appear today.

While some tell stories of continuity in favour of allowing circumcision, others tell stories of progress that may advocate a ban. An extract from a letter to the editor is typical of a line of argument most often found, within the material, in texts written by ordinary members of the public: "Now the state will accept that sound baby boys can have parts of their genitals removed when their parents so decide based on medieval religious practices" (Henriksen, 2014). The president of the Norwegian Humanist Association presents a similar line of thought in slightly different words: "I don't understand how Norwegian parliamentarians, in 2014, can allow a several-thousand-year-old, outdated ritual…" (Johnsrud and Nordland, 2014).

Rather than emphasising the value of continuity with the past, a break, or at least necessary transformation over time, is emphasised. Once again those who favour a ban or age limit employ arguments that resemble ideal Protestantism. Breaking away from tradition is at the centre of Protestantism's origin as a historical reality and even more as founding myth. More than most other religious traditions, Protestantism diversified and spread through conscious breaks with the past as new churches were formed. Berger's quintessential Protestantism, Pentecostalism, is among the most obvious fruits of a series of such breaks. However, unlike the secular narratives of progress which the president of the Humanist Association represents, Protestant breaks with the past are not only directed towards the future. Each break or reformation does not claim to be the beginning of something entirely new, but rather a return to an original state of purity that tradition has spoiled. From an outsider's perspective, Protestantism's relationship to tradition and history and its narratives of change and progress may be proof of religion's plasticity and openness for change. However, Protestant self-understanding presupposes that Christianity has an unchanging essence or core that can be reclaimed, and that each break with history is also a return to Christianity's earliest history.

Protestantisation – privileging sacred scripture and established authorities

All the examples of protestantisation that have been identified so far have been found among those who argue for a ban (or age limit) on circumcision. In a few cases, those opposing a ban make *explicit* accusations that their opponents are too indebted to a Protestant frame of mind. In most cases, it is a matter of recognising typically Protestant traits in the structure of the arguments. However, one of the few explicit allegations of undue reliance on Protestant understandings of religion is made in the opposite direction. Religion scholar Anne Kalvig claims that those who oppose a ban on circumcision are influenced by a Protestant tendency to essensialise religious traditions, to look for their immutable "core", and to seek this in sacred scriptures.

Kalvig has been the most active participant in the circumcision debate from among scholars of religion in Norway.[15] She is a strong proponent of introducing an age limit on male circumcision and sees the practice as similar to female circumcision (or female genital mutilation). Her emphasis on the importance of consent and a child's "right to its own self"[16] (Kalvig, 2014) (that is, the right to choose) is typical for the protestantised understanding of religion that I have explored above. However, Kalvig herself finds a Protestant bias precisely among those who oppose an age limit. She claims that the Protestant legacy leads to an essentialising view of religious traditions and an overemphasis on sacred scriptures and traditional (male) authorities:

---

15 Kalvig is the author or co-author of seven out of a total of 15 texts written by religion scholars in the material under investigation.
16 Norwegian, "barnet sin rett til seg sjølv".

With a classical definition of religion marked by Protestantism, in which religion is belief in spiritual beings with monotheism as the supreme example, it becomes difficult to foster good discussions on many important topics. It leads us to reproduce (certain) religions' official versions in which the life worlds of women and children, sensing, experiences, bodies, materiality and border areas, such as death, are excluded from view (Kalvig, 2016).

In Kalvig's view one of the most dubious consequences of such protestantisation is that it establishes a hierarchy among religious traditions (or practices that arise out of these) according to which such practices that have a basis that fits within a Protestant frame are protected, whereas those further removed from a Protestant mindset, are not. Practices that are expressions of "existential seriousness and conviction" (Kalvig, 2014) are worthy of protection, others are not. This approach, Kalvig claims, is sometimes coupled with a tendency to put emphasis on what the sacred scriptures say while attaching less importance to traditions that do not have a basis in recognised sacred scriptures. A concrete example of this is gender discrimination when female genital mutilation (for which there is no scriptural basis in any religion) is banned whilst male circumcision (prescribed by the Torah/Bible) is paid for by the public health service. This further deprives the observer of the ability to see that religions are flexible and constantly changing and that forces other than the traditional authorities may play key roles in creating new religious expressions. Kalvig is among those who frequently point to the development of alternative rituals within Judaism, seeing them as a viable option for parents if an age limit is introduced.

Kalvig's allegation of protestantisation (albeit without the use of this term) is closely related to the broader criticism of the world religions paradigm, criticism that has been influential in the religious studies discourse over the last few decades, most elaborately laid out by Masuzawa (2005). According to this view, the notion of world religions grows out of a Western, and more specifically Protestant experience with religion and imposes a Protestant frame of understanding onto a range of diverse (religious) phenomena. The world religions paradigm tends to organise religions in a hierarchy where those most similar to (Protestant) Christianity rank highest, and those traditions that are not considered world religions rank lowest. Equally problematical is the tendency to privilege the normative traditions as they are expressed by the religious leadership, which is also overwhelmingly male, over folk religion, heterodox traditions and "lived religion". Normative traditions will almost by necessity promote the notion that the tradition possesses a core and that being serious about one's religion is a question of being faithful to this core. The Protestant legacy will lead people to expect to find the basis for this core in sacred scriptures.[17] This way of thinking about religion has been challenged by research on "lived religion" (Ammerman, 2016), a research tradition that Kalvig identifies with.

The type of protestantised formatting of religion that Kalvig warns against is most often found among those who are positively inclined towards circumcision. However, very clear examples can also be seen in texts from those who agree with Kalvig regarding a ban. One such example is in the Ombudsperson for Children's official response to the first White Paper in 2011. One of her arguments in favour of an age limit presupposes a clear orthodox contra non-orthodox dichotomy when she says: "Nevertheless it is not the case that those who do not circumcise their children are not orthodox Muslims, if the Ombudsperson for Children has understood it correctly" (Norwegian Ombudsperson for Children, 2011: 8).[18] The phrase "if…understood correctly" indicates that the Ombudsperson assumes that there *is* a correct understanding of Islam which the Ombudsperson herself does not have the authority to decide.

Conclusion: Protestantisations?

Those who contribute to the debate on circumcision in Norway regularly rely on a specific formatting of religion. In some cases, the formatting is made explicit, but in the overwhelming majority of instances the formatting of religion is implicit and presumably unconscious: One simply assumes what religion is or ought to be and argues from this platform. Norway has been under strong Protestant influence for centuries, and there is every reason to expect that the understanding of religion that people bring to the circumcision debate is formed by Protestantism. In this chapter I have highlighted a number of instances of formatting of religion that fit well with the Protestant form. These are representative of patterns of argument that are prevalent in the 436 newspaper texts on male circumcision that are at the centre of my analysis. I have specifically focused on three typically Protestant understandings of religion that often underlie arguments in favour of banning circumcision: first that the "inner" religion is primary and "outward signs" are secondary and can be arbitrary; second that ideal religion is freely chosen and deeply held; and third

---

17 Very few of the 436 newspaper texts under study argue in favour of circumcision with direct reference to the Torah/Bible, but there are some examples. One is found in a short letter to the editor which quotes Genesis 17,12 as proof that circumcision is a covenant God has made with God's people, and concludes with an exhortation: "May God bless this nation so we do not come under the curse" (Lobekk, 2017).

18 Norwegian: "…like fullt er det heller ikke slik at man ikke er en rett-troende muslim hvis man ikke omskjærer sine guttebarn, hvis Barneombudet har forstått det rett".

that true religion can (and even should) break with accumulated tradition and thus be able to change. These understandings of religion are closely related and share the assumption that religion has a core or essence of ideas and convictions. The fourth type of Protestant religion formatting – identified as such by one of the participants in the debate, Anne Kalvig, concerns where this core or essence can be found, namely in sacred scriptures and through its authorised interpreters.

Identifying typically Protestant traits in the debate is not proof of a causal relationship. However, the suggestion that there is such a relationship has been made at various points, also within the material I have studied. In addition to Ervin Kohn and Anne Kalvig, whose analyses I have discussed in some depth above, anthropologist Tordis Borchgrevink reflects on the Protestant influence on the circumcision debate in a newspaper interview in May 2017: "In such religions as Islam and Judaism the relationship to God is found in rituals and actions, whereas the Lutheran faith has made the relationship into a matter for the inner self" (Borge, 2017).[19] This reflection sums up well what we mean when we use the term protestantisation.

There are, however, a number of ambiguities in the application of the presumed Protestant religion format that I have also pointed out. One refers to the fact that examples of protestantisation are hardly ever found in interventions by official representatives of the majority Lutheran church, but seem to thrive amongst those who otherwise signal no specific affinity to the Protestant tradition. This may correspond well with the further observation that the instances of protestantisation I have identified do not primarily correspond to Lutheran theology, but rather to the theology of the more radical branches of Protestantism, notably Pentecostalism, which in Berger's analysis of protestantisation represents ideal Protestantism. However, some of the examples of the formatting of religion that I have looked at go further than even Pentecostal theology. For example, the expectation that Jews can substitute an entirely new ritual in place of circumcision severs the relationship between sign and signified more radically than any Protestant Eucharistic theology, and when choice is emphasised in an analogy with "baptism of believers", the notion that the free choice should be given a conventional expression guided by tradition (the ritual of baptism) is out of sight. Lastly, when religion is expected to break with tradition or renew itself, the idea seems to be that something entirely new should be created, which is counter to all examples of Protestant breaks with tradition that always imply, at least in the self-understanding of those involved, a reclaiming of the past and return to a truer and more original tradition.

Should these observations lead to the conclusion that what I have identified as protestantisation in fact does not deserve this name? I think not. Their ambiguities and sometimes lack of correspondence with current Protestant norms rather alert

---

19 Norwegian: "…har inderliggjort gudsforholdet".

us to the fact that if we can show a causal relationship between the Protestant tradition and widespread current formatting of religion, such formatting has taken on its own life independent of lived Protestantism. Rather than expressions of Protestantism, they are as much expressions of a specific Protestant secularism.

Bibliography and material consulted

Ammerman, Nancy T. (2016). "Lived Religion as an Emerging Field: An Assessment of its Contours and Frontiers". *Nordic Journal of Religion and Society no. 2*, 83–99.
Berger, Peter (2007). "Pluralism, Protestantization, and the Voluntary Principle." In *Democracy and the New Religious Pluralism*, edited by Thomas Banchoff, 19–29. Oxford: Oxford University Press.
Borge, Arne (2017). "Verdifellesskap i folkevandringenes tid." *Vårt Land* (30 May).
Brekke, Torkel (2013). "Naiv tro på vitenskap." *Aftenposten* (29 October).
Henriksen, Tor E. (2014). "Religiøs vold mot barn." *Dagsavisen* (23 July).
Horsfjord, Vebjørn (2017). "Populærprotestanten: Nøysomhet uten gudsfrykt." *Kirke og Kultur 4*, 299–318.
Horsfjord, Vebjørn (2020). "Om skjæring – hva handler omskjæringsdebatten 'egentlig' om? En analyse av avistekster fra debatten om rituell omskjæring av gutter." *Din – Tidsskrift for religion og kultur 1–2*, 67–92.
Johnsrud, Nina and Nordland, Ester (2014). "Religiøst merket for livet." *Dagsavisen* (14 November).
Kalvig, Anne (2014). "Knivskarp toleranse." *Klassekampen* (10 April).
Kalvig, Anne (2016). "Spiritisme er levd religion." *Vårt Land* (20 February).
Kohn, Ervin (2013). "Omskjæring bra for barna." *Vårt Land* (21 December).
Lobekk, Rakel (2017). "Omskjering av guteborn." *Dagen* (22 May).
Masuzawa, Tomoko (2005). *The invention of world religions: or how European universalism was preserved in the language of pluralism*. Chicago: University of Chicago Press.
Ministry of Health and Care Services (2011). *Høringsnotat. Rituell omskjæring av gutter*. Oslo.
Norwegian Ombudsperson for Children (2011). *Høringssvar om rituell omskjæring av gutter*. Oslo.
Nyhus, Håvard (2017). "Omskjæring og seksuell nytelse." *Vårt Land* (23 March).
Rønsen, Arild (2017). "Omskjæring og dåp." *Klassekampen* (17 March).
Våge, Ingjerd (2014). "Kniver om omskjæring." *Vårt Land* (12 April).

Erlend From

Chapter 6: None of the Above. Yet a Tad Protestant?

1. Introduction

This paper will discuss how Norwegian 'nones' reflect and neglect Lutheran Protestantism. Based on my research,[1] the intention is to analyse how nones in Oslo relate to Lutheran Protestantism and the Church of Norway and how that might affect their own (lack of) a worldview. Is there such a thing as a Protestant format of (non-)religion in this material?

1.1 Methodological approach

My research is focused on non-religious identities in Oslo, interviewing women and men in the 30–40 age cohort who in one way or another do not identify with religion and religiosity. I address this populous as 'non-religious identities',[2] well aware of its intrinsic diversity and with an aim to address this diversity in an adequate manner. Despite the diversity, there are some commonalities: They are reluctant to identify with any – both religious and secular – worldviews, and they take their own non-religious identity for granted; it is perceived as a natural and default position, while religiosity is conceptualised as an active choice of belief.

In this chapter I will discuss how non-religious identities in Oslo relate to religion in Norway, and with an emphasis on whether there is a Protestant format of religion in these trajectories. The 'religious backdrop' can be conceptualised in various ways that are related to different concepts of religion. When methodologically conceptualising Protestantism in my material, I make a distinction between material and immaterial dimensions of (Protestant) religion. The material dimension relates to explicit references to church, Christianity, Islam and so on; occasions where the informants and/or myself make explicit references to institutionalised forms of religion during the interviews. By immaterial dimensions I refer to the discursive elements of religion that are better understood as *how* my informants *talk about*

---

1 This chapter is based on my empirical research on 'non-religious identities'. The project has been approved by NSD – Norwegian Centre for Research Data. All names are pseudonyms.
2 I prefer to address the field as 'non-religious identities' rather than 'non-religion' because of the singularity of the latter. By referring to 'non-religious identities' instead of 'non-religion' we are better equipped to circumvent any misconception that we are addressing anything like a homogenous group.

religion and religiosity in general terms. The latter occurs perhaps most explicitly when the informants describe 'less problematic religion' and on other occasions where there is a certain construct of 'good' and 'bad' religion.

The notion of 'formatting religion' and 'Protestant format' is inspired by Olivier Roy (2013) who identifies a 'process of formatting Islam into a Western model of relationship between state, religion and society'. In this chapter, Roy's notion of 'formatting religion' is seen in conjunction with 'protestantisation' (see Berger 2004) when asking if there is a Protestant format of religion represented by nones in Oslo.

According to Roy (2003: 16–17), 'formatting religion':

> [p]ushes a faith community to organise itself along the dominant paradigm. For example, imams are now expected to represent the community – which they do not do in traditional Islam – as priests or rabbis do (…). The consequence of this formatting, both through the personal practices of the believers and through state pressure and action, is to put Islam within the same paradigm as the other religions.

'Protestantisation' is a concept suggesting that the influence of Protestantism goes beyond confessional discourses such as church and theology, which for instance – and relevant for this chapter – affects how also non-protestants conceptualise religion and religiosity according to a Protestant framework. According to Peter Berger (2004: 79), protestantisation has more to do with the 'social forms of religion' than it has to do with 'theology or piety'. Protestantism has within its regional hegemony in north-western Europe become an archetype of religion. This chapter intends to test that hypothesis by asking whether nones in Oslo make use of a 'Protestant format' when engaging in conversations about religion.

Relevant features of the Protestant format for this article are religion as private matter, individualisation of faith, secularisation (as differentiation) and the shift of authority from church to individual. Under the discursive hegemony of the Protestant format, Protestantism is constructed as 'rational religion' (see Hurd 2008, on 'Judeo-Christian secularism') that nurtures social cohesion and supports the state, democracy and human rights. It is to a certain extent inseparable from the state apparatus and to the idea of nationhood. It is *good* religion; a rational way of being religious.

The Protestant format is materially represented by the Church of Norway, as well as by the 'Christian element' in Norwegian law, politics and institutional practice (e. g. religious education). In contemporary politics in Norway, this concept of religion occurs frequently with references to 'our Christian cultural heritage' (*vår kristne kulturarv*) as core values in need of various forms of protection. The notion about heritage hence has a material origin that is discursively represented by various actors who include it in narratives about national identity. This is the religious backdrop, the hegemony that Norwegian nones traditionally challenge, which has been loudly represented by the Humanist Association since the 1950s.

The purpose of this chapter is to discuss whether my informants have cut their bonds to 'Protestantism' completely or if there is still a Protestant discourse traceable in their narratives. 'Protestantism', 'protestantisation', 'Protestant format' and similar terms are invoked in my study as analytical tools to better understand how nones in Oslo make sense of their own non-religiosity, as well as how they perceive the religious other. One strategy of doing so has been to analyse how my informants talk about (non-)religion and (non-)religiosity; what is deemed 'good' and 'bad' religion in their narratives and to investigate where such evaluations might come from. It is in this way that the 'Protestant' element is included in my research, and there is no doubt that there is a Protestant (and also secular) format of religion that is portrayed as preferable, or perhaps we should say 'less problematic' when talking to nones in Oslo.

Furthermore, I find it useful to distinguish between material and immaterial representations of Protestantism in my analysis. Put briefly, material representations refer to the actual presence of Lutheran Protestantism in Norway, e. g. through the Church of Norway, and references to Lutheran Protestantism/Christianity in politics and law. Immaterial representations are represented more discursively, for instance in the manner in which my informants *talk about* religion and religiosity.[3]

1.2 Non-religion and cultural contingency

There seems to be consensus among scholars of non-religion that the very research object – *non-religion* – is a culturally contingent phenomenon, meaning that non-religious identities are primarily constructed against dominant religious formats and institutions. For instance, Phil Zuckerman (2008) explains Scandinavian non-religion and its indifferent character by pointing, inter alia, to characteristics of the former state churches. In similar fashion David Thurfjell (2015) analyses Swedish nones in the light of Swedish Christianity and thereby labels it a post-Christian society, while Alexandros Sakkelariou (2016) shows how Greek atheists construct their identities in conflict with their Orthodox backgrounds.

In general terms, it is suggested that non-religious identities are constructed in dialogue and conflict with majority religions on local levels. Johannes Quack (2014; Quack and Schuh 2017) addresses this adequately by drawing on Bourdieu's

---

3 The idea of material and immaterial power structures is inspired by Furseth and Repstad's (2003) concept of material and non-material structures in society (*materielle og ikke-materielle samfunnsordninger*).

theories on 'discursive fields'.[4] This means that non-religion is better understood and analysed in its conflict and dialogue with other sociocultural fields, in which fields of religion are highly relevant. In similar fashion, Beaman and Tomlins (2015) argue that the key to understanding different atheist identities across the globe is the different host societies that the respective individuals experience and relate to, which is echoed by William Stahl's (2015) claim that non-religious identities are shaped differently in Protestant and Catholic contexts.

Hence, researching nones in Norway assumingly should include Lutheran Protestantism as a discursive field that Norwegian nones touch ground with. That being said, research on non-religion cannot rely on this relation alone as it risks neglecting other cultural impulses that might be – and arguably are – equally important for understanding how and why people live their lives in various ways 'other than religious', to use Lois Lee's (2012) least common denominator for 'the non-religious'.

'Non-religion' is probably equally diverse as the term 'religion', and includes 'anything which is primarily defined by a relationship of difference to religion' (Lee 2012:131). More specifically: 'Non-religion is any position, perspective or practice which is *primarily* defined by, or in relation to, religion, but which is nevertheless considered to be other than religious' (ibid). Hence, non-religion incorporates a vast range of positions, from the utterly indifferent to the 'spiritual not religious', as well as affirmative atheists.

I argue, moreover, that non-religious worldviews might as well be informed and inspired by other sociocultural phenomena and are not necessarily constructed solely in opposition to their most immediate religious counterparts. For instance, my research shows that Lutheran Protestantism is not the only format that dominates conceptions of religion when interviewing nones in Oslo.

1.3 Addressing non-religious identities in Oslo

Measuring religious affiliation, identifications and the alike is a difficult task in Oslo and in Norway as elsewhere. In Norway there will be geographical variations of (non-)religiosity, and the lack of representative census data leaves researchers to make mere estimations when attempting to count the population's (non-)religiosity. That being said, we are, nonetheless, not completely lacking in data to make some qualified estimations.

---

4 'Discursive fields' refers to the methodology of Quack (2014; 2017) who makes good use of Bourdieu's field theory. In Quack's methodology, Bourdieu's 'relationalism' (Quack and Schuh 2017: 11) is instrumental for the acknowledgement 'that every field has a co-constitutive outside', which means that non-religion 'is more or less dependent on a relation with the religious field' (Quack and Schuh 2017: 11).

In the outset, Norway appears quite solidly Christian, with approximately 70% of the population affiliated with the Church of Norway (*Statistics Norway* 2018), but it is difficult to draw any conclusions from these statistics, for several reasons. Most important is the automatic enrolment into the Church of Norway on birth (if one of the parents is a member), a practice that has now been stopped, as since October 2018, the Church of Norway no longer has access to the Population Register. Until recently, it has been rather complicated to opt out, and when disaffiliated, many individuals have experienced being re-enrolled without their consent. Hence, passive and involuntary memberships are fully possible in the Norwegian context.[5]

It is also worth noting that the non-affiliated are the second largest group, and perhaps more importantly, the fastest growing group in Norway (Botvar and Schmidt 2010; Taule 2014). Moreover, if we look specifically at Oslo, the numbers tell yet again a different story: 49.4% of the population of Oslo (70% on the national level) are members of the Church *(Statistics Norway* 2018), and baptism rates are significantly lower in Oslo (30.9% - *Church of Norway* 2017) compared to rest of the country (53.6% - *Church of Norway* 2017).

Oslo scores low on religious belief, practice, belonging and affiliations compared to the rest of the country (Botvar and Shmidt 2010; Høeg and Gresaker 2015). At the same time, Oslo is far more diverse in terms of faith and worldviews and has a longer history with diversity than the rest of the country, at least with the 'new' diversity that is. By new diversity, I refer to the presence of significant numbers of 'other religions' than Christianity, such as various branches of Islam, Hinduism and Buddhism. These are sometimes labelled 'immigrant religions' (Leirvik 2016) due to increased immigration from 'non-Western' societies since the 1960s.

Hence, researching 'nones' in Oslo brings more religions and religiosities to the table than the traditional Lutheran Church of Norway that is so often associated with national identity. In fact, for my age cohort, especially for those who are born and bred in Oslo, Islam and Muslim identities are often more natural points of reference when talking about religion in general terms. One might suggest that this is a mediatized phenomenon (Hjarvard 2008), but my informants also demonstrate that they are more likely to have Muslims in their (extended) networks than Christians in Oslo, therefore when asked about religion and religiosities their points of reference are quite often their relationships with Muslim friends, colleagues and former classmates. In a Norwegian context I believe this is rather unique.

---

5 For further discussion, see From (2018): 'Who's the Master of None?', www.nsrn.net, URL: https://nsrn.net/2018/02/21/whos-the-master-of-none/ (accessed 17 Jan. 2019).

2. Distance and disinterest

My study shows that for this specific demography in Oslo, 'Protestantism' as represented by the previous state church of Norway (dissolved 2012) is not a significant actor that non-religious identities are shaped against. This is most explicitly illustrated when I ask my informants about the Church of Norway:

> S: Generally speaking, even though I'm against the church, but… but I also see that – at least in Norway – that the church is rather moderate compared to a lot of other countries, so I'm not that concerned.
> E: So the church doesn't resemble the destructive power structures you associate with religions in general?
> S: Well if we're talking about Jehovah's Witnesses and all that, then yes, but uhm… no, the church in Norway isn't like it was 1000 years ago, I guess.
> E: No.
> S: and it's.. it's much milder and I think that it had to change in order to survive.

An interesting feature of Susannah's (40) answers regarding the Church of Norway is how she swiftly moves on to address other organisations as well, e. g. Jehovah's Witnesses. Now, to be fair to Susannah it is important to note that she actually makes a distinction when saying that the Church of Norway is not *that* 'problematic' as it is purportedly moderate, mild and possibly perceived as less of a destructive power structure than the Jehovah's Witnesses in the example above.

For others, like Kaja (39), it is apparent that the Church of Norway is yet to be forgiven for past and present conservative attitudes towards women and sexual minorities:

> [I]t needs to become more open. If not, people will withdraw from this nightmare that doesn't… that very recently didn't want to marry gay couples, right…

That Kaja mentions gay rights when talking about the Church of Norway is representative for my sample, and is amongst the issues that my informants have in common: that religious traditions and institutions are criticised for past and present discrimination against women and minorities, in which the oppression of homosexuals is an important issue that is non-negotiable: An eyesore that, based on my respondents' opinions, the church will not be able to shed itself from in any foreseeable future.

I find it striking in my material that my informants do not contextualise much when asked about religion and religiosity, which I think is due to the lack of personal encounters with religion and religiosity, and therefore, Christianity and the Church of Norway are hardly addressed. There is a clear position of no relationship to the church:

> I'm not really well informed about it, the Church of Norway isn't something I take any interest in, but isn't it quite alright?
> Frank (34)
> Nah, I don't know, they're alright I guess… but I think they have too much power and receive too much state funding. The funding increases while membership decreases, which doesn't make sense… uhm… and they have a privileged position in Norwegian society that I don't appreciate.
> Kristine (32)

Both Frank and Kristine express little knowledge about the church other than expecting that 'it's not too bad'. Kristine worries about the politics of religion in Norway, which still privileges the church, but that's a matter of principle to her as an active member of the Humanists, regardless of the church's content, attitudes and so on. Also when asked about religion in general, it is striking that Frank makes no specific references:

> Well… it's indeed…. [Religions] They're there you know and I guess I occasionally think about it, wondering how long they're supposed to be there really, not that I'm… I'm not a militant atheist you know, but I think indeed that ehm… I do in fact tend to think that religious people are a bit… that it's a bit silly in a sense… that they're stupid, it's not completely like that because I know that many are quite intelligent, but I don't get it you know, so I… think a bit along those lines hehe.

2.1 How can you tell?

It is also worth mentioning that there might be something about the 'Protestant format' that is part of the story here: How can you tell a Protestant from a non-Protestant among your colleagues for instance? Note that my operationalisation of 'Protestant format' here is a mode of religiosity that is strictly reserved for the private sphere. In this respect, I admit that my material has more to say about my informants' perception of their peers than being solid evidence for the (non-)religiosity of the networks involved. 'My friends are like me, they're non-religious' is a typical quote from my material. Obviously, on many occasions that is probably true, but quite often I have experienced that there is more uncertainty to such statements than what is apparent at first glance. For instance, Tina (34) cannot really talk about her mother's (ir)religiosity:

Dad's very religious ehm… Mom eh… ehm… yeah… she's begun attending church during Christmas. Something we didn't do when I grew up, but it's not something extensive you know. (…) There's never been much talk about belief. (…) Ehm, but we're baptised and we had our confirmation you know… I think that's just something you do, you know.

This sequence with Tina reveals quite a few interesting things about perceptions of religiosity amongst nones in Oslo. Note that Tina makes a distinction between *belief* and *practice* (Church attendance during Christmas). To be truly religious in this narrative, *belief* is the crucial threshold. She cannot talk about her mother's (non-)religiosity because they are yet to have *that* discussion about *belief*. There is a rather obvious element of belonging here, but it is not deemed sufficient (enough) for 'Tina' to recognise her mother as religious. This is arguably a Protestant take on religion; it is close to irrelevant what you do and how you affiliate, it all boils down to your personal belief, belief is what distinguishes the religious from the nones. Another factor that feeds into the same conception is 'Tina's' notion of rituals as 'just something you do'. Religious rituals (baptism, confirmation, wedding and funeral) are not (anymore) tokens of religious identity and belief; they are services provided by the church for religious and non-religious identities alike and it is down to the involved persons' (dis)belief whether the ceremonies are deemed religious or not. Here it is worth mentioning that 'Tina' is from the coastal area in the north, in the county of Finnmark. When she grew up, and probably still, opting for secular alternatives to rites of passages involved long commutes:

E: Was there a realistic alternative to go to for confirmation – at the Humanist Association?[6]
T: No, I'm from a very small place. I would have needed to travel one hour by car each way ehm… to a place where I knew no one… yeah.

Tina proves the monopoly over faith and worldview held by the *Church of Norway*, especially when we take the vast country into consideration with its long distances between towns (especially in the northern regions). In other words, the church has become a natural place to go for Norwegians for marking significant transitions in life. However, this is about to change and, in Oslo, it has changed already, as illustrated by Per (34) below:

---

6 According to the Norwegian Humanist Association, 17.4% of Norwegian 15 year-olds opted for the Humanist alternative to the confirmation ritual in 2017 (www.human.no, URL: https://human.no/nyheter/2017/mars/rekordtall-for-humanistisk-konfirmasjon/). On the national level, 57.9% opted for confirmation with the Church of Norway (*Statistics Norway* 2018a).

E: (…) Are you or have you ever been a member of a faith or worldview community?
P: Yeah, I've had indeed civil… civil [Humanist] ehm… confirmation so I might have been… confirmed as a humanist you know… Ehm, when my father died we chose to bury him using a guy from the Humanist Association without really being aware of what they represent as such, but eh… but instead of proceeding with a priest to bury him we chose something else you know. But, no. In mysterious ways, I've been registered with the state church at some point, and I tried to opt out several times ehm… and finally managed and I've got the letter confirming this hanging on the wall, hehe.

Per was born, bred and still lives in central Oslo, and it is apparent in his answer above that he describes a rather different context than Tina. Per shows little personal relationship with the Humanist Association, but due to their mere presence in Oslo and his obvious disaffection with the church, he has turned to the Humanists twice for carrying out rites that traditionally have been monopolised by the church in Norway, and in many places still are, as pointed out by Tina. Taking my respondents' statements at face value, there is little evidence to suggest anything like Grace Davie's (2007) concept *vicarious religion* or that there is a *religion as a chain of memory* (Hervieu-Léger 2000) at play in these narratives. Instead, nones in Norway make use of church rituals more pragmatically and if there are secular (Humanist) alternatives, an increasing proportion of the population opt for it, which is the case in Oslo for instance, where there has been a significant decrease in baptisms in recent decades (Høeg and Gresaker 2015).

2.2 What is 'Protestantism' to nones in Oslo?

'Protestantisation' and 'Protestantism' are terms suggesting that the Reformation brought about changes that had impact beyond churchly discourses and beyond fields relating explicitly to religion and religiosity. Nowadays, 500 years down the line, due to secularisation, the Lutheran Protestant Church of Norway has arguably lost its former position as a dominant cultural and social power in Norway. Formally, it has ceased to be the state church, but with its privileged position in the Constitution it remains 'the established church' (The Norwegian Constitution, Article 16).[7] Nonetheless, it can be argued that there are remnants of Protestantism

---

7   §16: *All inhabitants of the realm shall have the right to free exercise of their religion. The Church of Norway, an Evangelical-Lutheran church, will remain the Established Church of Norway and will as such be supported by the State. Detailed provisions as to its system will be laid down by law. All religious and belief communities should be supported on equal terms* (The Constitution of the Kingdom of Norway, English translation: https://www.stortinget.no/globalassets/pdf/english/constitutionenglish.pdf, accessed: 31 Jan. 2019).

in society, both at the state level (laws, politics and institutions) and at the grassroots level, in terms of identity, belonging, culture and tradition.

2.3 A Protestant hegemony?

In the Norwegian case, the dominant religious format of Protestant Lutheranism is a natural point of reference when talking about (non)religion with nones in Oslo. The religious format is relevant for the analysis in two different ways. First, the ways of being religious within the Protestant framework have been rather uncontested in Norway since the Reformation: Defining religion and religiosity is subordinated to the Protestant way of practice and belief, which is represented by different actors that in diverse ways influence the Protestant discourse. Such actors can in the Norwegian case be various stakeholders, such as the Church of Norway, politicians, religious actors, experts on religion, media representations, as well as legal experts and institutions of law. With strong traditional ties between church and establishment (state, politics, law and institutions), Protestantism holds a hegemonic position in the Norwegian landscape of faith and worldviews. This means that there purportedly is a Protestant hegemonic discourse of religion; an immaterial power structure that is fixed in our language and conceptualisations. When we talk about religion and religiosity, the Protestant format is an archetype that affects how we think and talk about religion and religiosity in general, also when there are 'other religions' than Lutheran Protestantism involved, as per Roy's (2003) notion of formatting Islam in Europe. Second, there is a material presence of Lutheran Protestantism mainly represented by the Church of Norway and its position within the constitution and other actors representing the majority religion.

As Norway until recently has been rather culturally homogenous, religion and religiosity have been synonymous with Protestantism in the Norwegian public. This is not, however, commonly referred to as such. Because of the aforementioned homogeneity, my informants do not tend to specify denominations (i. e. 'Protestants' and 'Catholics'), but rather refer to 'Christianity' and 'Christians'. The Protestant format of religion and religiosity has become an archetype of what *being religious* really means, and ought to be. This fashion of conceptualising religion and religiosity is *doxa* (Bourdieu 1993); a discursive meaning of religion and religiosity that affects our perceptions, but rather unconsciously due to its discursive hegemony (Foucault 1999).

Meanwhile, other religions and religiosities – differing from the protestant format – threaten the social order and challenge democratic virtues and human rights. They are perceived as *bad* religion, for e. g. being led by authoritarian actors, institutions and social structures that allegedly limit freedom of the individual and threaten social cohesion. An idealisation of a secular public sphere is key here and generates scepticism against the public display of religion and religiosity, which possibly is the reason why expressions of religious difference (e. g. through apparel and dietary customs) are debated over and over again. Such dichotomising perspectives on various religious formats arguably breach boundaries between the religious and the non-religious, meaning that the conceptualisation of religion (the *good/bad* construct) has become part of the language of greater society, including the non-religious populace. I argue that this is one dimension of protestantisation that is discursively traceable in my conversations with nones in Oslo.

2.4 Challenging the hegemony

Asking a non-religious person in Norway about religion would traditionally be equal to asking about the (Lutheran Protestant) Church of Norway. This is no longer the only immediate association as Norway – Oslo in particular – has become significantly more diverse due to immigration, on the one hand, and due to an increase in non-affiliation and unbelief on the other. More religious visibility in the public sphere (including the media) does not imply that the masses are not moving in the opposite direction, i. e. becoming more secular in their personal beliefs and practices (Botvar 2010: 11). On the contrary, researching nones is in many cases acknowledging that:

> [I]n many parts of the world the old story of secularisation remains salient. In these places, traditional religiosity continues a steady decline and what is called "subjective secularity" – unbelief and non-affiliation – continues to expand (Lee 2015: 2).

Research (Høeg and Gresaker 2015) shows that there is a correlation between urbanisation, pluralisation and secularisation in Norway. The population of Oslo shows less affiliation with the church; they are less likely to baptise their children and they demonstrate scepticism towards the church based on political issues, in which gay rights and the membership system are crucial (Ibid). My study shows that for many young adults in Oslo today, the first-hand experience with religiosity is likely to be represented by Muslim acquaintances rather than Christian ones. Additionally, I assume that different forms of non-religion have globalised – New Atheism[8] being the most obvious example – which possibly has led people to address religion in more general terms than referring only to the dominant religious format on the local level. Perhaps most importantly, religion finds itself at the centre of global

---

8 'New Atheism' refers to worldviews, ideologies and antagonism against religion represented typically and associated with the likes of Dawkins (2006), Dennett (2006), Harris (2004; 2006) and Hitchens (2007). The 'movement' is hallmarked by a strict materialistic worldview in which any religious discourse is incompatible with science.

media attention in the post 9/11 era. That being said, the discursive hegemony of Protestantism in the way we talk about religion and religiosity in Norway is probably something that is fixed in our language and will not disappear overnight even though the whole conversation about (non)religion has changed under the influence of global networks.

Hence, it might be equally relevant to scrutinise how these identities are constructed in mediation between local traditions and 'global networks' that connect Oslo to the rest of the world, both materially and immaterially. We need to ask how these different actors might have an impact on non-religious identities in Oslo.

3. Monopolising values

The boundaries of material and immaterial power structures are often difficult to distinguish. And importantly, for the methodological approach of 'formatting religion' and to demonstrate the impact of a 'Protestant format' it is paramount to acknowledge that immaterial structures are likely to have a material origin. One way of approaching this is to think about how '[r]eligion may have generated political consensus and affected the emergence of different welfare states – through the institutionalization of religious countries' poor relief systems, and the secularization of these institutions' (Kahl 2009: 267). According to Kahl, in a perspective of *longue durée*, ideas and values from a Christian heritage might survive into late modernity, but in the shape of secular forms. In similar fashion, 'our Christian cultural heritage' is a term that frequents Norwegian politics, law and education. The use of the term implies that core values in society are of Christian origin regardless of their contemporary secular articulations. Moreover, the Christian heritage is presented alongside 'our humanist heritage' in the Constitution (Article 2):

> Our values will remain our Christian and humanist heritage. This Constitution shall ensure democracy, a state based on the rule of law and human rights.[9]

And the same wording is echoed in the Education Act (§1–1):

> Education and training shall be based on fundamental values in Christian and humanist heritage and traditions, such as respect for human dignity and nature, on intellectual

---

9 The Constitution of the Kingdom of Norway: https://lovdata.no/dokument/NLE/lov/1814-05-17?q=grunnloven.

freedom, charity, forgiveness, equality and solidarity, values that also appear in different religions and beliefs and are rooted in human rights.[10]

It is hard to decipher where the 'Christian' component starts and ends in these paragraphs as one can easily interpret the 'humanist' component as an integral part of the 'heritage and traditions' that are – as first mentioned – 'Christian'. On another note, actually encapsulating the 'humanist' component – and other flattering democratic and human rights values – referring to 'our Christian heritage' is a common practice in contemporary identity politics (Roy 2003) in which different political parties demonstrate the variety of contesting interpretations that play into this field. Perhaps the most evident example of such discursive struggles is manifested in the debates on immigration.

The Christian element in the Constitution is an echo from the past when church and state power were inseparable; when being Christian was inseparable from citizenship; when it was prohibited by law *not to* baptise your children (revoked in the nineteenth century) and when religious education was mandatory and an integral part of the national curriculum. This is the material past of state religion in Norway that today manifests more immaterially when politicians and other stakeholders refer to the nation's Christian heritage. The concept here is that the Christian legacy carries civilising elements that nurture social cohesion and democracy. For people who do not identify with the church it is arguably hard to distinguish what exactly such a Christian legacy resembles and is therefore addressed with caution, to say the least. In other words, there is an awareness of the discursive power exercised by actors who in one way or another call for the protection of 'our Christian cultural heritage' in Norway. And as I will explore below, such different discursive implications are indeed represented in contemporary politics in Norway.

3.1 In the eye of the beholder

In Norway, two parties use the term 'our Christian cultural heritage' rather differently to support their arguments either for or against restrictive immigration policies: The Christian Democrats argue that the Christian heritage promotes values of compassion (*love thy neighbour*), demanding that Norway *fling wide the gates* for those in need. At the other end of the scale, the Progress Party claims that liberal immigration policies are culturally unsustainable and essentially a threat to

---

10 The Norwegian Education Act: https://lovdata.no/dokument/NL/lov/1998-07-17-61?q= oppl%C3%A6ringsloven, for English translation of section 1: https://www.regjeringen.no/en/dokumenter/education-act/id213315/.

the Christian heritage.[11] In this sense both parties are important actors who tap into what Christianity means and represents in Norway. Hence, whether e. g. the Church of Norway or the Faculty of Theology for that matter likes it or not – both the Christian Democrats and the Progress Party are amongst the actors that through their associations put meaning into the term 'Christian' and are therefore part of the fields that the non-religious relate to when reflecting on religion/Christianity in Norway.

Despite their differences (inclusion as opposed to protectionism), the Christian Democrats and the Progress Party share something that is a key part of the purpose of this article: They assume that religion saturates the institutions of contemporary society through values that – in the Norwegian case – were introduced half a millennium ago. In other words, both parties perceive 'our Christian cultural heritage' as inseparable from liberal democracy and human rights, which is a mode of the Protestant format, and as rational religion (Hurd 2008) that Norwegian nones possibly relate to when constructing their identities.

This take on religion in contemporary society resonates with the argument against 'traditional' and positivist secularisation theories (i. e. 'a secularising modernity'), namely that secularisation stems from an inner ecclesial process, initiated by the protestant reformation, which is why Milbank (2010:55), for example, describes secularisation as 'a self-distortion of Christianity – primarily in Western Europe'. In a similar, but less negative way, Taylor (2007: 233) argues that the internal process of secularisation meant that authority changed hands with the Reformation – from Church to the individual – meaning that his concept *exclusive humanism* is not a contradiction to Christianity, but rather a related offspring. The same reasoning is at play when 'our Christian heritage' is associated with core values of democracy and human rights. However, these attitudes are not echoed by my informants. To them, the Christian heritage is less associated with flattering values of human rights and democracy:

> "It's patronising. Norway pretends to offer humanitarian salvation, saying 'oh, poor bastard who doesn't have much (…), come here and I'll show you the right path.' But it comes with a price. It's like, 'you are my investment. Therefore, you need to become what I want… to become like me'… It's an expectation of me to adopt a recognisable lifestyle, but if you break with that… if you cook strange smelling food… or if you perform rituals that

---

11 E. g. MP Christian Tybring Gjedde (The Progressive Party) in a TV debate April 2016: *The Progressives and the Christian Democrats are united in the belief in the family and the individual human being and – above all – the belief in the Christian cultural identity of our country. (…) The Progressives promote a restrictive immigration policy in order to preserve a Christian cultural identity.* [My translation] (www.nrk.no, URL: https://tv.nrk.no/serie/dagsnytt-atten-tv/201602/NNFA56020416, (accessed: 31 Jan. 2019).

are unfamiliar… expectations are broken and sanctioned by a mild form of aggression. Religion is addressed as the problem, but it's really about cultural differences. However, Christianity becomes the solution."
David (34)

David is an atheist, born Eritrean and a refugee who came with his parents to Norway at the age of one. Apart from his years of study in Tromsø, he has lived in Oslo his whole life. However, when asked about the cultural heritage of Christianity in Norway, which is referred to with the specific term – 'Our Christian cultural heritage' (*Vår kristne kulturarv*) – he invokes the language of his refugee background and unmistakably associates the term with immigration policies. In fact, David does not really reflect upon what the heritage consists of; instead he gives his association to the term and its usage, which in his opinion is utilised as a tool of intolerance and dominance.

While David gives his associations when asked to describe his perception of the Christian heritage, others are more substantive in their replies:

It's just a grand construction… I mean, it's uhm… Christian heritage… what do we mean by that? Is it Christianity in the 1650's? Is it the 18th century pietism? I mean, what is the Christian cultural heritage?! It's obviously a result of… of the Christian influence on Norway throughout the ages, but I don't know if burning witches is something we're supposed to… we're supposed to speak loudly about as part of our cultural heritage, but it is indeed [part of it] hehe… uhm… to me, it's the same as national romanticism or Norway as nation so to speak… that too is a construction… what're Norwegian values? They're so many different things…
Martin (33)

On one level, Martin – another self-declared atheist in my study – does the same as David when deconstructing the term to reflect upon its usage when questioning its legitimacy as something that is supposed to unite and reflect Norwegian identity. On the other hand, he differs from David as he immediately examines the literal content of what the term possibly implies. To him it is too vague, too artificial and too loaded with undignified connotations to serve as the unifying term it intends to be. In fact, he dismisses the whole concept of consolidating Norwegian values in one singular concept. In this he implies – as does David – that the term splits rather than unites.

For another interviewee, Michael (39), a Soviet born atheist, the Christian heritage is – to my surprise – something that needs to remain in our conscience and be protected:

> E: [...] Article 2 in our Constitution declares that its fundamental values shall remain our 'Christian and humanistic heritage'... What do you think about that?
> M: I think it's a good thing 'cos... uhm... it reflects the hist... the historical process... uhm... we had the Christian legacy, then humanism was added and so on. So... I think it's a good thing. As good as it gets, it could have been better, but... it's discussed – as far as I know – heavily whether... when Norway was Christened, whether Norway became... if it became a more peaceful society, that people became more equal before the law, and then there's people saying 'no, no, it was much better during the Viking age, that the laws were better and so on... But... I'm not sure what to believe, but perhaps no one can be certain about that, but in the outset I think... the more solid the rule of law the better, and if the law respects Christianity and all that, I'm happy, the further away from Sharia at least...

Michael reveals early in the interview that he is a strong atheist, and he shows rather intolerant attitudes towards the religious other, but when asked about Christian heritage – his tone changes. To my surprise, he seems more tolerant of the Christian legacy, but it is notably led by an aversion against a less attractive alternative, which in his opinion is the Muslim legacy of Sharia. Here, he addresses a dichotomy that has achieved a certain acknowledgement in the public debate: that the presence of Islam in Europe threatens culture and democracy, which calls for protection of 'our own cultural heritage' against the rule of Sharia. Hence, it seems as if Michael affiliates with the Progress Party's use of the term 'our Christian cultural heritage' in identity politics; a token of 'good religion' in need of protection from 'bad religion' (Islam). This is also emphasised by Roy (2003: 11):

> [M]any rightists oppose Islam because they consider that Europe is first of all a Christian region. Nevertheless, for most of them, Christianity has little to do with religious practices, it has to do with identity, not faith. Interestingly enough, many secularists are increasingly aligning themselves with the agenda of the Christian right by defining Europe as culturally Christian. But the Christianity they are defending is not a faith, it's an identity.

Hence, we see that the terminology 'our Christian cultural heritage' does not carry univocal interpretations and that different actors contribute to different associations.

4. Non-religion in its glocality

Traditionally, secularisation and urbanisation are seen as closely related processes and the general impression has been that urbanites are less religious than people in rural areas (Lee 2017: 135). It is commonly assumed that urban dwellers have not found 'new ways of being religious' in the city, 'but are rather entirely immersed in the material world, wholly preoccupied with their lives in the "earthly city"' (Lee 2017: 135, referring to Strhan 2015). But according to Lee (2017), these are, however, merely assumptions, and there is not a sufficient amount of empirical research on nones in urban contexts to support the assertions. Another issue is that most of the data to support the argument has predominantly been focused on rather explicit non-religious identities, such as 'the sceptical, materialist, existential humanist, existential secularist, alternatively spiritual or any others with non-traditional existential world views and cultures' (Lee 2017: 135). In other words, there is a lack of research addressing *other* non-religious identities, which for instance could be the 'average none' in Oslo, who is arguably less concerned about religion and religiosity than those who are formally affiliated with, for example, the Humanist Association.[12]

Lee argues that sociological research on the global city, such as Sassen (1991), has revealed that instead of being predominantly secular, the global city is instead super-diverse and the location 'in which the visibility and influence of religion has resurged' (Lee 2017: 136). This is also true for Norway, but it is not the same as asserting that there is a religious revival or that there is strong evidence of anything like the 'de-secularisation' suggested by Peter Berger (1999). Berger's revision of his own secularisation theory and similar critiques of 'grand secularisation theories' for being essentialist and positivist have gained solid ground within the sociology of religion in recent decades. A revision of the purported causality of modernisation and secularisation indeed has its place, but the last decades' increased research interest in the field of non-religion has arguably shown that the influence of the likes of Berger (1992) and Casanova (1994) probably has generated another phase of 'grand narratives' within studies of religion that are in the same need of revision as the theories they intended to rectify.

Lee (2017: 136) makes the same argument when pointing out that the post-secular school has not paid sufficient attention to non-religious identities in the global cities. By shifting the focus from the 'areligious' to the 'non-religious', Lee (2017: 136) addresses parallel movements with the 'growth of religion in the city, namely the rise and revitalization of overtly non-religious cultures within these spaces'. Even though Lee's (2015) research from southern England is in many ways incomparable to my own research in Oslo due to magnitude, history, sociocultural and political backdrop, I argue that the similarities in terms of globalised cities are strong enough to employ a similar framing of Oslo as a global post-industrial urban culture. Essential for such framing of a post-industrial and global city is

---

12 The Humanists are a minority of the non-religious populace in Norway even though the Humanist Association in Norway is relatively large compared to its sister organisations abroad.

its implications for demographic composition, for conduct of life and therefore how meaning, purpose and belonging are constructed. Sociocultural diversity is of course of great importance, including (non-)religious pluralism.

In the global city it is possible that the 'neighbouring discursive fields' that Quack's (2014) methodology is based on are less local and that the 'experience and relationship with the host society' (Beaman and Tomlins 2005: 5) is less significant. This is perhaps most prominent when conversing with informants of other cultural, ethnic and religious backgrounds than what is commonly associated with the 'host society'. For instance in my material, it is apparent that Tina (Kven), Haya (Syrian/Muslim), Michael (Soviet/atheist) and Susannah (Syrian/Muslim) bring more 'discursive fields' into their narratives than Norwegian Protestantism. Moreover, their global networks are intersected with local traditions that are also integral parts of their identity. The demographic diversity makes it highly problematic to assume homogeneity in relation to ethnicity, religion and other cultural parameters. No wonder why 'our Christian cultural heritage' is therefore hard to stomach for many of my informants.

5. Individualism and authenticity

Having no particular worldview category to identify with, Kaja expresses a certain content with a broad undefined identification such as 'non-religion' (an identification Kaja picked up upon when I introduced my study):

E: ehm, you describe yourself as non-religious ['ikke-religiøs']...
K: Yes, we should have a non-religious category here [in Norway]... or perhaps that's what you're about to establish?
E: Yeah, maybe hehe. But what does it mean to you when you're saying that you're non-religious?
K: As I said, I don't manage to choose [a worldview category], I don't want anything to believe in, I want to be free in terms of... what to think because to be locked immediately to... how to think about how humans came into being; what we're doing here; then everything is kind of thought for you. I want to... I have to be free to make up my own mind. (...) That's the reason, and also because I think many find comfort in it [religion] and that's wrong. You should not be religious because you find comfort and support externally, you're supposed to find that within yourself you know. (...) And people don't do that, because they lean on religion, they'll end up in heaven regardless of their fuck-ups along the way, I mean... that's not for me, I don't identify with it.

When talking about religion and religiosity, Kaja expresses a typical individualist character that has resonance with other interviewees as well. In my material, religion and religiosity are breaking with what I recognise as an ethic of authenticity (Taylor 1992); that *choosing* to be religious is perceived to compromise an individual's ability to make up her own mind by relying on an external authority. Moreover, within this framework religiosity is a sign of personal weakness and the incapability to make independent decisions and form opinions as it ultimately means that you sign up for and rely on a readymade package of ideas, morals and beliefs; a package that cannot be disentangled from its authority in which patriarchal and hetero-normative power structures are intrinsic.

> In my opinion 'spirituality' ['åndelighet']… eh… as a way of constructing a superstructure for people's life is positive at the end of the day, I mean these rituals that function as social support; to generate calamity (…). But the oppression ehm… of women in particular, and sexual minorities are vulnerable. (…) Also, I don't appreciate that people become like… religious for the sake of religion… I mean, if you sit on your own and are religious then for God's sake hehehe, pun intended, that must be allowed… I think… because that's something very personal and not anyone's business really… It's when systems… like ehm… The Salvation Army, I think they sort of do a fantastic job, but again they have a discriminatory view, which is not okay, and the missionaries… missioning eh… the Mission Association ['Misjonssambandet'] – I find that… I find that really disgusting.
> Tina (34)

During the conversation it is obvious that Tina is struggling to come to terms with religion, and the core of her ambivalence is her idea that there is initially nothing wrong with religion per se, but when people do 'bad stuff' in the name of religion, that troubles her. The discriminatory practices towards women and minorities and the religious other are what make religion difficult for Tina to digest.

Another interviewee, Ane (30), identifies as atheist, and her take on religion and religiosity is heavily influenced by her feminist view:

> Ehm… and from what I learnt about religion that I read with interest in the paper or in a periodical, I can't see… and I think that's pretty much from feminism, for instance that the interest for equality and queer rights, for instance, that it's hard to get why you'd want a religious conviction that… that doesn't support equality for all, for instance… so then it becomes… then I think it's wrong; it's the wrong way of doing stuff. To govern by… or to think that not everyone is worth the same, for instance… so that's indeed… perhaps that's latent in atheism, you know.

6. Yet a tad Protestant?

Despite these testimonies of unfamiliarity with the church and with Christianity in general, there is arguably a Protestant fashion of talking about religion that dominates my informants' take on religion and religiosity. I say *arguably*, for two reasons; first, because 'Protestantism', 'Protestant' and similar terminology is hardly mentioned by the interviewees (remember, the Protestant element is exclusively an analytical tool in my approach). Second, the notion of the Protestant format could easily have been replaced by 'secular'. The reason for that is that the same hallmarks for Protestant piety and the concept of religion are quite often – and perhaps even more so – associated with secularisation. On the other hand, many will – and probably rightfully so – argue that secularisation is a Western phenomenon, generally propelled by a shift of power from institution (church) to the individual, similar to and related to the individualisation of faith that the Reformation brought about; withholding the sanctity of the Bible over the church and the individual responsibility for pious living over loyalty to the clergy. The story is obviously more complex, but the main point here is that there are good reasons for understanding the processes of secularisation against a Protestant backdrop, which is why certain scholars (e. g., Milbank 2010) maintain that secularisation is a product of a Protestant framework and ideology.

The hallmarks I refer to above as shared features of the Protestant and the Secular relate first and foremost to the division between a private (religious) and public (secular) sphere. Within this context, religiosity ought to be private business and predominantly manifested as personal belief. In fact, within this framework religion is synonymous with *belief*, which is core to how the *Protestant format of religion* is operationalized in this chapter.

Following this line of argument, we might say that the increasing non-religious population in Norway is a bi-product of Protestantism (catalyst for secularisation); that the shift of agency and power from institution to the individual now is visible in a population that seems less affiliated with the church and is less prone to be socialised into religiosity than previous generations. Within this framework, religion – as belief – is conceptualised as something that is chosen rather than being understood in terms of identity and belonging: You choose to believe and not believing does not demand an active decision. It is rarely conceptualised as a social matter, perhaps unless you are part of various kinds of minority religion, either Muslim or Christian. It is rather conceptualised as a natural order of a mature and educated mindset.

Frank (34) puts it this way when asked about what he thinks is problematic with religion:

Ehm... to actually believe in... to kinda believe in specific things that uhm... that are unlikely hehe. We could proceed with other problematic stuff that might have negative impact on society like Catholicism and abortions and contraception and stuff like that, but I don't think much about that... I'm more concerned about why people choose to believe and how I find that weird and therefore problematic.

To Frank, religiosity is problematic because it marks a choice of believing in something that is (scientifically) unlikely. It is implicit in his answer that choosing religion is difficult to understand because it implicitly means that one is denouncing science. We get the sense here that with several rational options available, choosing religious 'superstitions' is difficult to comprehend. Implicit in these narratives, there is an interesting tendency to perceive non-religiosity as a natural and default position.

In similar fashion Kristine (32) refers to choice when reflecting upon her own atheism:

It means that I don't believe in any god, and that I think it's very weird that people do that [believe in God]. I think it's very puzzling that... someone in society today... being educated and all... (...) Uhm... I said earlier that I kinda don't understand why people believe, it's so spaced out... it's not comprehensible, but on the other side I understand perfectly well why people choose to believe when having a hopeless... uhm... everyday life and hopeless situation. That it gives hope and purpose to... perhaps lives that lack purpose in the outset. I understand it well if you live in extreme poverty and you kind of don't stand a chance of escaping it in this life... it's a bit dull if this is it in a sense, then it's nice to think that you eventually will end up in heaven and that things will be better there... Just hold on a bit longer and everything's gonna be just fine...

In Kristine's answer, choosing is synonymous with coping, which implicit in her narrative is senseless if your existential needs are covered. In this perspective, 'healthy' modernisation that grants existential security makes religion redundant, which is how Phil Zuckerman explains Scandinavian indifference to religion in *Society Without God* (2008). This also sits well with how Talal Asad (2003) theorises modernity as a Western political project in which secularism is an intrinsic part.

Discussing whether Zuckerman's analysis and reference to existential security is right is beyond the scope of this paper and my project in general, but I can confirm that this perspective holds strong ground with my informants and is depicted in the perception of religion as chosen (against all odds). It is a perception that something needs to go wrong if people are turning to religion, whether for purpose, explanation or comfort. Doing so in a 'well-functioning' society such as the Norwegian one is then a choice for the weak and the lost. My informants seem to proclaim typical modernist views on religion as a token of weakness, uneducated naivety and delusional comfort for various forms of deprivation:

> To me, religion is…a… not only a pillow to rest on… I think there's something very comfortable… really, religion is like an inflatable mattress. It's comfortable to rest on, and filled with nothing. Nice to lean on when things are not so cool, nice to play with, but uhm… I don't know what to say… Religion to me is just… it's just… something that directs your life because you're not able to control it yourself. A comfort zone to me.
> David (34)

Following this rationale, choosing to be religious – choosing to believe – is to consciously head down an irrational road while being well aware and informed about the irrationality of doing so. David finds amusement in this when hanging out with religious friends:

> I have a tendency to kind of tease a bit about it you know. Quite often… and it's like… it can be everything… like asking them to text Jesus and ask him to let us pass the nightclub line, 'you believe in him don't you?'… Stuff like that.

Now, this is obviously a casual joke among friends and does not need to be highly significant for David's overall perception of and feelings towards religion and religiosity, but at the same time it reveals how religion is perceived to be an irrational choice that David thinks breaks with a consensus in contemporary Oslo, that religious beliefs are abnormal and worthy of friendly mockery.

What makes these narratives a 'tad Protestant' is that religion and religiosity are predominantly conceptualised as 'personal beliefs', while identity and belonging are hardly addressed.

6.1 Religion is religion

A majority of my informants claim that it does not matter to them what people believe: whether it is something religious or not is purportedly not relevant, but only if – and this is important – belief remains in the private sphere. Susannah (40) remains faithful to her 'hardcore atheist' identity when asked about the religious other, meaning that she is rather uncompromising in her perception of the religious other – the Abrahamic religions in particular. She stands out in my sample with a relentless antagonism towards Islam. That is perhaps not surprising as Susannah is an atheist from an Islam-dominated community in Damascus, Syria, who has lived in Oslo the past 20 years. This shows the importance of 'neighbouring discursive fields' (Quack 2014; 2017) when aiming at understanding nones. Analytically we can add another field to Susannah's discursive landscape, referred to as 'Protestant format' in this paper, which is evident when answering the question about 'less problematic religiosities'. In this sequence, Susannah is favouring an archetype of religiosity that is arguably Protestant; something that is strictly to remain in the private sphere and not to occupy space publicly:

> Just keep it to yourself... ehm... and as long as your choices don't affect others, you can believe in God and Mohammad and the sun for that matter, I can tolerate that.

On the other hand, religion becomes a problem for Susannah when it is believed to challenge individual freedom:

> E: How about religion, generally speaking, can you say something about that, let's say we'll start with... do you see anything positive in religion – institutionally in particular?
> S: No... not in 2018. No, maybe there was a need for it 1000 years ago, but no. (...) What I see now, maybe religion can be unifying, but... but there's so much power in it, and... and perhaps I'm talking more about Islam uhm... that unifying power is also utilised in a negative and destructive fashion uhm... so no, I don't see anything positive in that, I really don't.
> E: If we're... it's related though, but how about negative sides to religion?
> S: Yeah, do you want a list hahahaha. I mean, it's destructive, it destructs eh... again I'm caught up with Islam, Islam's per definition... It means 'submission', it's... which to me is to give up on your right to think, to make up your own mind so... yeah, it's nonsense really.

Nearly all of the informants apply such a 'Protestant format of religion'. When describing 'less problematic religion', they echo a Protestant format: Religion ought to be a matter of personal belief and remain in the private sphere with little influence on social and public life. Moreover, religiosity is problematized for impeding independent thinking and therefore depicted as a threat to Taylor's notion of 'ethics of authenticity' (1992).

7. Conclusion

Actors of the Protestant format, and other actors that are local and global, (non)religious and completely secular are equally important, but incomplete if not seen in association when attempting to understand the formation of non-religious identities in Oslo. The Protestant format as a hegemonic discourse probably affects how non-religious and religious Norwegians perceive the religious other, but in a globalised and post-industrial environment there are other actors, such as style of work and how meaning and purpose are formed in new arenas that do not include religion – or any worldview for that matter, that are (at least) equally important for the social formation of non-religious identities. Nones in Oslo do not need to 'believe' in anything, which is illustrated by my informants' lack of identification with both religious and non-religious worldviews.

As demonstrated in this article, 'Protestantism' and related terminology such as 'protestantisation' and a 'dominating format of religion' are interesting analytical tools when exploring the formation of non-religious identities in Oslo. In the introduction, I asked whether there is a 'Protestant format of religion' at play in my material. The answer to that question is yes, but not without clarification. With respect to the narratives presented by my informants, it would be misleading to claim that the formation of their non-religious identities is primarily shaped in dialogue and conflict with the dominant format of religion in Norway, which is Lutheran Protestantism. However, I have shown that there are nonetheless reasons to say that there is a Protestant fashion of *talking about* religion represented in my material.

My argument is that the Protestant format seems absent in terms of material power structures, but it manifests itself immaterially. By that I mean that a 'Protestant format of religion' holds a hegemonic position – an immaterial power structure through language and conceptualisation of religion and religiosity – that has an impact on how nones in Oslo relate to religion in general. This means that non-religious identities are not predominantly formed against a Protestant backdrop, but the Protestant discourse is decisive for how informants *talk about* religion and religiosity.

To summarise, using Protestantism as an analytical category tells us more about how nones conceptualise religion than anything relating to their own (lack of) worldview and non-religious identity. Hence, there are reasons to believe that non-religious and religious identities alike engage with a Protestant discourse when talking and thinking about religion and religiosities and it is therefore plausible to conclude that there is a dominant format of religion in Oslo that is Protestant. This hegemony is predominantly operating within immaterial power structures. Material power structures of Protestantism are not difficult to identify in Norway (law and politics), but it does not strike one as a relevant 'discursive field' that non-religious identities are shaped against. On the contrary, my informants seem rather detached from the Christian heritage and are quite indifferent to Christianity, the church and so on when constructing their own (lack of) worldview.

Bibliography

Asad, T. (2003). *Formations of the Secular – Christianity, Islam, Modernity*. Stanford: Stanford University Press.
Beaman, L. G. & S. Tomlins (eds.) (2015). *Atheist Identities - Spaces and Social Contexts*. Cham: Springer International Publishing.
Berger, P. (1992). 'The Desecularization of the World: A Global Overview', Berger, P. (ed.) (1992): *The Desecularization of the World*. Michigan: William B. Eerdmans Publishing Company.
Berger, P. (2004). 'Christianity and Democracy: The Global Picture'. *Journal of Democracy*, Volume 15, Number 2, April 2004, pp. 76–80.
Botvar, P. K. and U. Schmidt (2010). 'Endringer i nordmenns religiøse liv'. In Botvar, and Schmidt (eds.) (2010), *Religion i dagens Norge – Mellom sekularisering og sakralisering*. Oslo: Universitetsforlaget.
Bourdieu, Pierre (1993). 'Site effects', in Pierre Bourdieu (ed.) *The Weight of the World – Social Suffering in Contemporary Society*. Stanford, California: Stanford University Press.
Casanova, J. (1994). *Public Religions in the Modern World*. Chicago: The University of Chicago Press.
Davie, G. (2007). *The Sociology of Religion*. London: Sage Publications.
Dawkins, R. (2006). *The God Delusion*. Bantam Press.
Dennett, D. (2006). *Breaking the Spell: Religion as a Natural Phenomenon*. New York: Penguin.
Foucault, Michel (1999). Diskursens orden [L'ordre du Discours 1971]. Oslo: Spartacus Forlag.
Furseth, I. and Repstad, P. (2003). *Innføring i religionssosiologi*. Oslo: Universitetsforlaget.
Harris, S. (2004). *The End of Faith: Religion, Terror, and the Future of Reason*. W.W. Norton and Company.
Hitchens, C. (2007). *God is not great*. London: Atlantic Books.
Hervieu-Léger, D. (2000). *Religion as a Chain of Memory*. New Brunswick: Rutgers University Press.
Hjarvard, S. (2008). *En verden af medier – Medialiseringen af politik, sprog, religion og leg*. Fredriksberg: Samfundslitteratur.
Hurd, E. S. (2008). *The Politics of Secularism in International Relations*. New Jersey: Princeton University Press.
Kahl, S. (2009). 'Religious Doctrines and Poor Relief: A Different Causal Pathway'. In Van Kersbergen, K. and Manow, P. (eds.) (2009), *Religion, Class Coalitions and Welfare States*. Cambridge: Cambridge University Press.
Lee, L. (2012). 'Research note: Talking about a revolution: Terminology for the new field of non-religion studies'. *Journal of Contemporary Religion* 27 (1): 129–139.
Lee, L. (2015). *Recognizing the Non-Religious. Reimagining the Secular*. Oxford: Oxford University Press.

Lee, L. (2017). 'Godlessness in the Global City'. In Garbin, D. and Strhan, A. (eds) (2017), *Religion and the Global City*. London: Bloomsbury Academic.

Leirvik, O. (2016). *Religionspluralisme. Mangfald, konflikt og dialog i Norge*. Oslo: Pax forlag.

Milbank, J. (2010). 'A Closer Walk on the Wild Side'. In Warner, M., Vanantwerpen, J. and Clahoun, C. (2010), *Varieties of Secularism in a Secular Age*. Cambridge: Harvard University Press.

Quack, J. (2014). 'Outline of a Relational Approach to 'Nonreligion''. *Method and Theory in the Study of Religion* 6 (04) 439–469.

Quack, J. and Schuh, C. (2017). 'Conceptualising Religious Indifferences in Relation to Religion and Nonreligion'. In Quack, J. and Schuh, C. (eds.) (2017), *Religious Indifference. New Perspectives from Studies of Secularization and Nonreligion*. Zurich: Springer.

Roy, O. (2013). 'Secularism and Islam: The Theological Predicament'. *The International Spectator*, Vol. 48, No. 1, March 2013, –5 19.

Sakkellariou, A. (2016). 'Forms of Atheism in Contemporary Greek Society: Beliefs, Practices and the Formation of the Atheist Identity'. *Annual Review of the Sociology of Religion*, 2016, pp. 161–179.

Stahl, W. A. 2015. 'The Church on the Margins: The Religious context of New Atheism'. In L. G. Beaman & S. Tomlins (eds.) (2015), *Atheist Identities – Spaces and Social Contexts*. Cham: Springer International Publishing.

Taule, L. (2014). 'Norge – et sekulært samfunn?', *Samfunnsspeilet*, 1/2014, pp. 9–16.

Taylor, C. (1992). *Ethics of Authenticity*. Cambridge: Harvard University Press.

Taylor, C. (2007). *A Secular Age*. Cambridge: Belknap Press.

Thurfjell, D. (2015). *Det gudlösa folket. De postkristna svenskarna och religionen*. Stockholm: Molin & Sorgenfrei Akademiska.

Urstad, S. (2018). *Ikke-religiøse i Norge. Sosiologiske analyser av individer uten religion*. University of Agder. (Doctoral thesis).

Zuckerman, P. (2008). *Society without God: What the Least Religious Nations Can Tell Us about Contentment*. New York: New York University Press.

Online

The Church of Norway (2017). 'Årsrapport 2017 (Annual report 2017)'. www.kirken.no, URL: https://kirken.no/globalassets/kirken.no/om-kirken/slik-styres-kirken/kirkeradet/2018/mars/aarsrapport_for_den_norske_kirke_2017.pdf (accessed 17 Jan. 2019).

The Constitution of the Kingdom of Norway: Grunnloven. www.lovdata.no, URL: https://lovdata.no/dokument/NLE/lov/1814-05-17?q=grunnloven (accessed 17 Jan. 2019).

Dagsnytt Atten (2016). www.nrk.no, URL: https://tv.nrk.no/serie/dagsnytt-atten-tv/201602/NNFA56020416, (accessed: 31 Dec. 2019).

From, E. H. (2018). 'Who's the Master of None?', www.nsrn.net, URL: https://nsrn.net/2018/02/21/whos-the-master-of-none/ (accessed 17 Jan. 2019).

Høeg, I. M. and Gresaker, A. K. (2015). 'Når det rokkes ved tradisjon og tilhørighet. Nedgang i oppslutning om dåp i Oslo bispedømme', *KIFO Rapport 2015:2*. www.kifo.no, URL: http://www.kifo.no/wp-content/uploads/2016/09/KIFO-Rapport-2015_2-Nar-det-rokkes-ved_-til-web.pdf (accessed 05 March 2019).

The Norwegian Education Act. www.regjeringen.no, URL: https://lovdata.no/dokument/NL/lov/1998-07-17-61?q=opplæringsloven (accessed 17 Jan 2019).

The Norwegian Humanist Association (2017). 'Rekordtall for humanistisk konfirmasjon', www.human.no, URL: https://human.no/nyheter/2017/mars/rekordtall-for-humanistisk-konfirmasjon/ (accessed 17 Jan. 2019).

Ipsos MMI (2015). *Færre nordmenn tror på Gud*. www.mynewsdesk.com, URL: http://www.mynewsdesk.com/no/ipsos-mmi/news/faerre-nordmenn-tror-paa-gud-110842 (accessed 24 Feb. 2016).

Statistics Norway (SSB) (2018). www.ssb.no, URL: https://www.ssb.no/kultur-og-fritid/statistikker/kirke_kostra (accessed 17 Jan. 2019).

Statistics Norway (SSB) (2018b). 'Kommunefakta, Oslo' www.ssb.no, URL: https://www.ssb.no/kommunefakta/oslo (accessed 17 Jan. 2019).

Trygve Wyller

Chapter 7: Can Protestants Resist Christianism?

Scandinavian Creation Theology As Political Theology

Introduction

The American sociologist Roger Brubaker (Brubaker 2017) recently proposed the category "Christianism" to describe a significant position in immigration policies. The Christianist is a person who claims that "we" need to avoid an influx of refugees and migrants because they threaten the established Christian values in the West. These values are freedom of speech, a secular way of arguing politically, gender equality and the balance of power. The Christianist wants to defend the "Western" values with walls, security policies and deportations.

This article will discuss whether, and how, radical Protestants can resist the Christianist category. In a liberal context, the category "Christianist" is an obvious candidate for "bad religion", the non-generous, the populist, the rigid and so on. Populist/Trumpian simplifications are the unambiguous representations of the Christianist. The question is, however, how this position is resisted. The thesis in this article is that it is not good enough to refer simply to one or another Christian interpretation, saying things like "generosity is part of basic Christianity" or "all people are equal in the eyes of God".

One might, however, defend "our values" in a more reflected way than by simplifying proclamations. In the following, the issue of establishing a Protestant position beyond the secular/religious binary will be the main focus. The Christianists, on the other hand, are nurtured from this binary. They claim to represent the Christian/religious position by pursuing explicit Christian values and enhancing a direct link between this specific faith and politics.

The thesis in this article is that it is inherent in Protestant Christianity to resist this secular/religious binary. The Christianist challenge is that they narrow what Christianity is and reduce it to a few restricted topics. But that breaks with the core of Christianity, which believes in a God that is there for all people, not just some people. In a theological context this means that the Protestant tradition I will elaborate on is the Scandinavian Creation Theology (SCT) (Gregersen, Uggla and Wyller 2017; Gerle and Schelde 2019). The SCT position argues why theology must reflect and pursue social issues and politics so that the discourse and practices include all people, not only those who call themselves Christians. This is why the SCT claims to contribute to a theology beyond the secular/religious binary, and why this position is considered to be the one that promotes a Christianity that is the opposite to the Christianity of the Christianists. In the following, some narratives from the immigration context will be used to illustrate this position.

Kirkenes

The first case is from the very far north of Norway, from Kirkenes in the county of Sør-Varanger, and in the border zone to Russia. In the early winter of 2016, many Syrian refugees entered Norway in the arctic cold at the Russian-Norwegian border. The Norwegian authorities were first perplexed and then acted with strong legal measures. The Syrians were first placed in provisional camps in the Kirkenes area, and then soon after, many of them were returned on buses back to Russia.

During these hectic days with strong restrictive policies and deportation many local people acted with anger and resistance. Spontaneous counter actions blossomed, heavily covered in both the national and international media. Some people drove into Russia to drive the refugees the last miles into Norway. Others tried to take refugees out of the provisional camps. On one occasion, a group of refugees was taken into church asylum in the Lutheran church in Kirkenes.

The church warden in the area later talked about how she was then confronted with an impossible dilemma: in Norway the local authorities own the church buildings. The church warden, very often a person from the congregation, is a municipal employee, and this warden was trapped between two loyalties: One to the local and legal authorities and one to the congregation and the people of faith.

For more than 20 years there has been an agreement between the Lutheran Church of Norway and the Norwegian government concerning church asylum. Church asylum is not a legal right in Norway, which means that the police can enter the churches to arrest anyone who has sought refuge there. However, the agreement regulates when this can and cannot be done. The church has admitted that church asylum is not automatically protected by the law, but the authorities have also admitted that, when cases of church asylum arise, the police will not immediately enter the church to make an arrest. Instead, the agreement points to the aim of having a positive dialogue to arrive at an acceptable solution.

Being aware of this, the church warden was quite worried as she knew that the police could approach her at any time and to ask for the key to the church. She had decided that if the police called, she would then hand over the key. She really had no alternative due to her status as a municipal employee.

Her solution to her dilemma was both simple and shrewd: Instead of waiting for the police to call, the church warden took the key with her and drove to her cottage which was a two-hour drive away. She left her cell phone at home so no one could reach her. This was, no doubt, an act of silent civil disobedience, but first of all an act performing another kind of Christianity. Loyalty to the law is one strong aspect of Lutheran faith, the car ride into the isolated area was, of course, confirmation of that loyalty. While confirmed, it was still, however, contravened by symbolizing another kind of faith beyond legality and formalities.

Gothenburg

The Lutheran Bergsjøen congregation is located just north of Gothenburg on the Swedish west coast. Bergsjøen is a suburban area, a new residential area for white working-class Swedes. In the most recent decades immigrant families have moved into the area. Today 80 per cent of the people living there are non-ethnic Swedes, and a consequence of this is that the Lutheran congregation of Bergsjøen has diminished. The ministers and the board of the congregation therefore decided to open the church for people from different denominations. The services today are held in different languages and with different liturgical practices. The congregation engaged in being a learning and teaching centre for old and new immigrants, establishing language courses, cooking and food courses, cooperating with the local school to support dropouts and so on.

In addition to these locally based practices, the congregation also cooperates with the Rosengrenska organization, which has been established, for example, by doctors, nurses, lawyers and social workers to improve and enhance the social and health situation of irregular immigrants in Sweden (Wyller 2014, 2016). The Rosengrenska volunteers come to the church every Wednesday evening, and it then turns into a clinic for irregular immigrants. At 5.00 p.m. they appear at the church and sit in in the cafeteria waiting to have consultations and meetings with immigrant families and friends. The project, one of the most remarkable of its kind in northern Europe, has attracted much attention in recent years.

There are no laws or procedures in Sweden regarding church asylum and churches as sacred spaces. In a Protestant context, the church is not a sacrament and therefore the police can, in theory, enter any church and arrest the people they want. But in practice they have not, to my view, done this.

The Bergsjøen/Rosengrenska project is not the only project where churches aim at supporting (irregular) migrants beyond the accepted national policy. There are innumerous projects of the kind all around the world. What is specific for Bergsjøen is the explicit cooperation with the non faith based organization Rosengrenska, and that the project has had a remarkable location in the Swedish (and sometimes Nordic) public. In this way the Bergjøen/Rosengrenska project represents a practice where Lutheran churches challenge and (sometimes) provoke the established juridical situation in the field of migration. The project opens question on whether Swedish politics and legal decisions have the ethical quality one should expect.

An ethics (and a theology) beyond the legal

In Norwegian politics most parties have adopted the slogan "strict, but just" to express their immigration policies. The slogan was probably initiated by the right wing and populist Progress Party (*Fremskrittspartiet*), but is today accepted by all parties except the far-left. At their recent Party conference, the Labour Party dropped the word "strict" and proposed a new phrase "consistent, just and humane". But in a comment, one Labour leader claimed they were still promoting a "strict, just and humane" immigration policy.

The refugee conflict in Kirkenes was reconciled after weeks of political struggle. The government dropped their intention to bus all the refugees into Russia and accepted processing all cases and individuals according to UN practice and expectations. A large number of the refugees were granted asylum and are today living in various regions in Norway. The people who took action during these hectic days are now back in normal everyday life, but the symbolic power that these days invoked still has impact and remains an issue worthy of reflection and discussion.

As we saw above, currently, leading Nordic politicians from the ruling parties claim that they favour an immigration policy that is "strict, but just" (*streng og rettferdig*), whereas the Labour Party's new phrase is less rigid. However, the intention remains the same.

The concept "just" refers to procedures, not to individual encounters. What is to be just is that people applying for asylum or a residence permit are entitled to procedures that are the same for everyone. Each refugee has the right to expect to undergo the same procedure as all others. This means that people who are granted asylum or residence permit will know that they are all on the same level. Moreover, on the opposite side of the coin, people who are denied asylum or a residence permit will accept that the decision is just, as only those who fulfil specific criteria will have the right to residence.

The politicians argue in the tradition of Max Weber and his distinction between "an ethic of responsibility" and "an ethic of ultimate ends" (Weber 1991). Even if Weber's famous pamphlet, *Politics as a Vocation*, is now more than a hundred years old, his theory still explains how many people argue ethically in the field of politics. I do not believe that the politicians following the strict, but just slogan are aware that they are following Weber, nor is it important if they do or not.

> We must be clear about the fact that all ethically oriented conduct may be guided by one of two fundamentally differing and irre- concilably opposed maxims: conduct can be oriented to an 'ethic of ultimate ends' or to an 'ethic of responsibility'. This is not to say that an ethic of ultimate ends is identical with irresponsibility, or that an ethic of responsibility is identical with unprincipled opportunism. Naturally nobody says that. However, there

is an abysmal contrast between conduct that follows the maxim of an ethic of ultimate ends—that is, in religious terms, 'The Christian does rightly and leaves the results with the Lord"—and conduct that follows the max- im of an ethic of responsibility, in which case one has to give an ac- count of the foreseeable results of one's action (Weber 1991 p. 120).

Nevertheless, Weber's distinction is helpful to understand why politicians choose to use the word "just". "Just" refers to a procedural and legal justice, following the rules established by political decisions and bureaucratic implementations. They do not at all mean "just" in the sense that one should follow a policy where all people are treated with the same dignity because they are created by the same God.

"Just", in the slogan "strict, but just", does not refer to that kind of justice at all. On the contrary, Weber contrasts the procedural "just" with what he calls "an ethic of ultimate ends" and connects that ethic to "the Christian". This means that the choice is between the responsible ethic which is concerned about the outcome, and the (Christian) "ethic of ultimate ends" that "does rightly and leaves the results with the Lord". Translated into everyday discourse, Weber is distinguishing between the procedural ethic that is oriented towards specific goals and a Christian ethic that is not concerned about specific goals, but leaves them to "the Lord".

Nevertheless, the cases from Kirkenes and Bergsjøen are not at all covered by such kinds of interpretation. When the church warden leaves for her cottage in the wilderness and the Bergsjøen congregation joins a project, which challenges democratic decisions in Swedish politics, they represent a different ethic than the one applied by Weber.

One interpretation is that the church warden and the Bergsjøen minister reflect what the Danish theologian K.E. Løgstrup has called the ethical demand (Løgstrup 1997). For Løgstrup, as for his Swedish colleague Gustaf Wingren, it was decisive that the demand coming from the neighbour was a demand to everyone, to Christians, atheists, Muslims, humanists, everyone. The "universal" character was, in Løgstrup's and Wingmen's interpretation, the only theologically acceptable interpretation. Since God was a God for all humans, that is, for many more humans than there are Christians, the ethical demand relates to all people, not to Christians alone.

The other aspect of Løgstrup's ethic is that the ethical demand coming from the neighbour is a demand that very often transcends politically decided procedures. The ethical demand is beyond and more than the procedures, more than the legal. The reason is that the ethic develops from an encounter, whether it is a personal or a contextual one. In all cases, the encounter is what develops the ethical demand, not the opposite; the encounter shall apply what has already been accepted in political and academic processes.

One might say it was this kind of political ethic that was implemented by the church warden. By taking the key and leaving for the remote cottage with no cell phone, she responded to the ethical demand arising from the encounters with the Syrian refugees and at the same time tried to avoid the established procedural justice. She obviously applied another ethic, one not concerned with the legal aspect, but more concerned with a demand for humanity beyond the it. This is the reason why she felt her action to be somewhat fragile, knowing that as a public employee, her job is to comply with the established and democratically decided procedures.

Nonetheless, by narrating the story and reflecting on it, one sees intuitively that the church warden was into something important and decisive. She connected another ethic, one that differed from Weber's "ethic of responsibility".

This is even more present in Bergsjøen. What is fundamental here is that the congregation presents an ethic that is far removed from what Weber calls a (Christian) "ethic of ultimate ends" that "does rightly and leaves the results with the Lord".

The congregation is absolutely not leaving the results with the Lord. It support the project, which aim at supporting people, who do not have a permit stay in Sweden. "The Lord" has no share in this at all. The congregation's ethic is not an ethic of irresponsibility, it is an ethic that presents a different responsibility. One could call this a responsibility towards the other instead of a responsibility towards the law.

Bearing this in mind, one sees why the slogan "strict, but just" is definitely confusing and misleading. The concept of justice in the slogan is first of all a justice of following the law and established procedures. The justice in the church warden's and the minister's actions is a justice arising from the encounter with the other, one that is more than an encounter with the law.

Based on this comparison, one might say that the difference between the two types of ethic comes from the disharmony between the sources of the two ethics, whether they are primarily procedural (the ethic of responsibility) or practical (starting with the encounters of the church warden and the minister). Both from an ethical as well as from a theological perspective, this is a difference of high significance. The theological difference is, in the context of the argument in this chapter, the most radical. However, in order to grasp the importance of this, a few more ethical reflections might deepen the argument.

Encounters, empathy

The phenomenologist and feminist Sara Ahmed (2000) is among many phenomenologists that give encounters decisive significance. In doing so, Ahmed criticizes the influential philosopher Emmanuelle Levinas. For Levinas the other is absolutely unreachable, different, and therefore unable to be connected to. Ahmed's point is that whatever the intention might be, there is a tendency to "fetish" the Other in Levinas, because he underscores the connectivity that has already been established between the other and myself and between the other and ourselves.

According to Ahmed, the others are already there, connected to us through touches, smells and voices, the sensibilities that we cannot but recognize. So the other is not a distant "fetish", the other is perceived and already impacts us through that embodied perceiving. The encounter is never just a social meeting; something precedes the concrete and what precedes it are such perceptions as "hearing and touch". Ahmed, also positively, relates to Levinas: "… Levinas introduces the notion of exposure, or as I would have put it, touchability, as the condition of signification or saying, as that which makes it possible to be for others, before being" (Ahmed 2000, 154).

The touch and the hearing are, then, part of the foundations for encountering the stranger as neighbour and the starting point for important ethical reflections on the Kirkenes and Bergsjøen cases. The church warden felt the arctic temperature on her own body and from that sensibility was already connected to the even more endangering artic temperature in the bodies of the bicycling Syrians. Being in Bergsjøen church every Wednesday afternoon means to be in the middle of all the non-Nordic smells. The sense of the smells is there as soon as you enter and before anything is spoken. Ahmed's embodied phenomenology deepens the practical ethic of the church warden and the minister. It opens an interpretative window to understand why the practical ethic needs to be an embodied ethic of sensibilities.

A further elaboration on this same area of phenomenology beyond the procedural comes from the Danish philosopher Dan Zahavi. In recent years he has (Zahavi 2014) focused on whether something called empathy exists and how such a phenomenon may be characterized. The decisive point is that empathy presupposes otherness, and that this empathy cannot but be embodied. Zahavi's context is the critique from both analytical and postmodern researchers. They do not recognize empathy as anything else but pure subjectivity. Zahavi argues convincingly against this. Empathy is much more than just an internal emotion. Rather, empathy implies that there are other bodies outside one's own self. Empathy has to do with the way I react in my body to other fellow human beings' embodied situations. When we express empathy it presupposes that there are some real others outside me. The existence and embodied presence of the other is sensibly experienced by me. Through my senses I become aware of the other's presence and embodied situation before I communicate my experiences in language or react to the other practically. Empathy comes from this first original encounter where my sensibility is shaped through the awareness of the other's body.

It is no wonder that one of the project leaders in Rosengrenska once summarized the experience of being exposed to all this in this way: "You feel rather naked"

(Wyller 2016). The emotion of being naked comes from the total exposure to others and others' exposure to yourself. Empathy, for Zahavi, presupposes the existence of others because it is exactly the awareness that something outside of me requires my presence and challenges me to a response, that is decisive. Empathy and otherness are closely connected.

The other (sometimes subversive), non-Christianist, Protestantism

What is striking with the church warden and the Swedish congregation cases is that their interpretative significance is connected to phenomena that are not necessarily conventionally "religious". First of all, there is the embodied, emotional awareness and exposure to, and of, others. Nevertheless, there are also seemingly trivial things like driving a car, possessing a key, failing to answer one's cell phone, locating a mobile clinic, and so on.

Bearing this in mind, the conclusion is there are two opposing and contesting profiles of Christianity emerging in the immigration field. The Christianist is the one who upholds the religious/secular binary, whereas the non-Christianist Protestantist (embodied in the church warden and the minister) acts and reflects beyond the religious/secular binary. The basic experiences from the encounters, the primacy of sensible embodiment and the empathy that develops from these embodied encounters are significant characteristics of the non-Christianist Protestant position.

Nevertheless, we also need to add one more characteristic, and that is how the non-Christianist practices respond to ethical demands beyond the legal and the procedural. We see this both in the case of the church warden and the case of the minister. Their activities respond to demands coming from encounters, not from the law or from conventional rules of everyday procedures.

From the Christianist point of view, these characteristics must lead to the conclusion that the non-Christianist Protestant is not Christian at all. Based on the elaborations presented in the introductory part of this chapter, that is absolutely not the case. The non-Christianist cases can be interpreted as presentations of a Protestant/Scandinavian (Lutheran) creation theology (SCT). The core of SCT is exactly that God is present but hidden when the ethical demands from the others are responded to. This is why the religious/secular binary needs to be bypassed. It does not address the fact that there is another presence of the transcendent.

This hidden presence is not meant to be a colonial effort to make all persons Christians. The opposite is true. It is meant as the contradiction to the Christianist. There is a Christianity that does not use religion for a political purpose. There is a Christianity that trusts the presence of the transcendent also within human encounters and empathy, also when the response is beyond the law.

The Christianist position is a position that is explicitly political. There is good reason to call it a political theology of the right. The upholding of a religious/secular binary is the main characteristic of this political theology. The genuine Christian needs to be protected in order to maintain the basic values of society.

The non-Christianist Protestant represents a potential political theology as well. But also as political theologist the non-Christianist argues exactly the opposite of the Christianist. The non-Christianist Protestant performs Christianity when it supports and pursues values that can be shared beyond confessions, beyond the religious/secular and (sometimes) beyond the legally accepted. There are, of course, other variations of Christianity. But the contradiction between the Christianist and the non-Christianist presented in this chapter might be one of the most significant disharmonies within contemporary Christianity.

Bibliography

Ahmed, S. (2000). Strange Encounter. Embodied Others in Post-Coloniality. London: Routledge.
van Den Breemer R., Casanova J., Wyller T. (2014). *Secular and Sacred? The Scandinavian Case of Religion in Human Rights, Law and Public Space.* Göttingen: Vandenhoeck & Ruprecht.
Brubaker, R. (2017). "Between nationalism and civilizationism: the European populist moment in comparative perspective". In Ethnic and Racial Studies, 40:8, 1191–1226.
Gerle, E., Schelde, M. (2019). American Perspectives meet Scandinavian Creation Theology. Uppsala: Svenska Kyrkans Forskningsenhet.
Gregersen, N.H., Uggla, B.K., Wyller T. (2017). Reformation Theology for a Post-Secular Age: Løgstrup, Prenter, Wingren, and the Future of Scandinavian Creation Theology, Göttingen: Vandenhoeck & Ruprecht.
Løgstrup, K.E. (1997). The Ethical Demand, Notre Dame, Notre Dame University Press.
Sander, H.J., Villadsen K., Wyller T. (eds.) (2016). *The Spaces of Others – Heterotopic Spaces. Practicing and Theorizing Hospitality and Counter-Conduct beyond the Religion/Secular Divide.* Göttingen: Vandenhoeck & Ruprecht.
Weber M. (1946). Politics as a Vocation. Reprinted from Max Weber: Essays in Sociology. New York: Oxford University Press.

Allen G Jorgenson

Chapter 8: Sensual Protestations: Luther, Løgstrup and the Promise of the Senses

Introduction

Protest is a perdurable phenomenon within religious traditions as certainly as is affirmation. Both emerge from a vision for the well-being of the world, a community, and/or an individual in light of an ultimate conviction. This deeper conviction is the driver for these, and calls forth at various times both affirmation and protest.

As noted in the introduction to this book, the notion of Protestantism receives both substantive and procedural interpretations, and the latter is of special interest in this collection insofar as "concepts are continuously subject to formation, contestation and negotiation, the reformation and protestantism quickly dissolve into vague and shadowy fields of discourse." (See "Introduction" above.) Behind, or beside, this play with concepts is the interplay between some sort of a teleology, or ultimate vision and certain facts on the ground, ever evolving and rich for procedural examination. In this chapter, I will explore an instance of this interplay when the facts are not so much on the ground as in skin and what it wraps around, asking what protest has to do with the body, and how this plays out in our reading not only texts, but bodies.

The religious phenomenon of protest can be given secular dress in the modern era because of the construction of the "religious" as a category used to describe what concerns belief in contradistinction to what is secular, which concerns what is removed from belief. This distinction takes leave of the ancient description of the religious and secular as internal to the corporate life of belief, wherein "religious" was used in reference to "anyone living under canonical vows of poverty, chastity and obedience in a community and under a rule." (MacGregor, 1991: 533), Secular clergy, by contrast, were not "bound by religious vows" but were "subject to the bishop under whose jurisdiction they exercises their priestly duty." (MacGregor, 1991: 564).

Within the paradigm of Christendom in the West, some priests were secular and some religious but all belonged to the church, which essentially encompassed the empire. The divorce of this ancient distinction of the secular and religious within unity was also accompanied by a schism of the body politic from the idea of a corporate belief, and parallels in interesting ways the privatization of religion. Both the divorce of the secular from the religious, and the privatization of religion accompanied an enlightened view of the body as mechanistic, rather than formed by the soul, as per Aquinas following Aristotle, for instance (Taylor, 2007: 330–31, 554). The body hereby then functions as a cypher for nature, and both – body and nature – are in need of domestication. The body needs to be tamed, and nature needs to be reined in under the aegis of an enlightened and decidedly dispassionate, reason.

The present work protests such an understanding of the body and its flesh, in which our sensuality is problematized along with nature itself.[1] In so doing, I draw upon Luther and a school of thought developed by Lutheran thinkers in the mid-20th century, who responded to an emerging Barthian theological paradigm that they felt did severe disservice to the theological topic of creation, or nature. I leverage this theology of creation in service of a reappropriation of the body and its sensuality.[2] Regin Prenter, Gustaf Wingren, and Knut Løgstrup are key figures in a movement entitled "Scandinavian Creation Theology" (SCT) which sought to protest this Barthian approach with a robust theology of creation, which they found in the thought of Martin Luther, the so-called Father of Protestantism. It is my contention that this attention to creation facilitates an appreciation of the body itself, which I use to protest the problematization of the body, flesh and sensuality.

In part, in what follows I explore an instance of Protestants protesting another Protestant in the conviction that creation—and with it, the body itself—is ripe for theological rumination. My concern regarding Christian antagonism toward the body is echoed by many sources both within and external to Christianity, and is especially clear in feminist and Indigenous voices. SCT is a particular instance of this dissatisfaction with Christian antagonism toward the body and nature, and is under exploration in the present work, especially as it emerges in the thought of the Danish theologian/philosopher Knut Løgstrup. What follows, then, is an instance of a constructive theology, drawing lessons from the Protestants Luther and Løgstrup and applying these to consider the possibility of a sensual protest, attempting to discern a bodily revelation such that flesh and blood become a site for encountering ultimate insights. Of course, this reading of the flesh does not dispense with the need for some sort of a self-reflective hermeneutic in reading such insights, nor does it disregard traditional sources, nature more broadly construed, reason and other religious traditions—all which may be generative for theological insight. It might be said that the present essay reflects Protestantism in a non-essentialist modality, and so is an instance of a procedural predilection shaped by the fact that

---

[1] In a sense this is nothing new – the platonic antipathy to the flesh being one example of its problematization in the past – but still, the contours of the problem of the flesh are differently received and considered today.

[2] It is beyond the scope of this chapter to survey or adjudicate this claim. Barthian scholars may well protest that Barth has a solid theology of creation. I am simply mindful of this critique of Barth as a backdrop for what follows.

"observers are always situated, that they rely on influences from their surroundings and that their perceptions are informed by different motivations which change over time." (See Introduction above.) And so, when one considers frequent critiques of Christianity's antipathy toward the body, it cannot be understood in isolation from the particular, and ever evolving, nature of this faith in a western context. Christianity's shape in the west is, in varying degrees, dependent on its Protestant iterations, and so an understanding of the body cannot be imagined in the West in abstraction from Protestantism.

Charles Taylor, in his *Sources of the Self*, gives a backdrop for this in providing a genealogy of modernity that draws some significant lines between Luther's understanding of vocation and the arrival of the secular by way of the Enlightenment. Here he underscores the positive sides of Luther's understanding of vocation, which correlate to the undoing of a hierarchical view of the cosmos and the affirmation of the ordinary (Taylor, 1989: 218) . This resulted in a loosening from "older moral horizons," as he notes in *The Malaise of Modernity* (Taylor, 1991:3). Luther's understanding of vocation allows the ordinary to be the site of divine service, and so prepares the way for later affirmation of the secular as important in its own right. A most important corollary of this development of the secular, as outlined in Taylor's *A Secular Age* is a reconfiguration of the role of the body in the modern imaginary. He distinguishes the porous self of the premodern era, a self that was subject to the forces of an enchanted world, with the self of the modern era that he calls the buffered self. What does this buffered self look like? We read

> The buffered self is essentially the self which is aware of the possibility of disengagement. And disengagement is frequently carried out in relation to one's whole surroundings, natural and social. (Taylor, 2007: 42)

This disengagement implied, after Descartes, a "rigorous distinction between mind and body." (Taylor, 2007: 131) This distinction has come at a high price. Feminists, in particular, have noted that it has resulted in the body being "colonized through the discursive practices of the natural sciences."(Grosz, 1994: x) Mary McClintock Fulkerson has noted how this has resulted in the commodification of the body. (Fulkerson, 1994: 95) In what follows I re-imagine the role of the body in a post-modern era as I engage the works of Martin Luther and Knut Løgstrup. I am also deeply indebted to my colleague and interlocutor Laura McGregor, who does qualitative research around the experience of mothers of medically fragile children. Her work has engaged philosophical and theological resources to explore the concept of the "lived experience" and questions of meaning. I might note that Laura is the mother of a recently deceased medically fragile son, Matthew who was unable to talk and was also in need of extensive care with significantly complicated health issues until his death on March 29, 2020 at the age of 21 years.

A book that has been influential for Laura and some of the work we have done together is *Carnal Hermeneutics*, edited by Richard Kearney and Brian Treanor. The intent of the work is to unsettle, if not undo a dubious legacy of the Enlightenment that is its purported distaste for the flesh. In the words of Kearney "Our wager in this volume is that such a move may help us better understand how we are constantly *reading* flesh, *interpreting* senses, and *orienting* bodies in passion and place even as we symbolize and dream. This is the task of carnal hermeneutics." (Kearney, 2015: 17)

As I have read and thought about this important work along with Laura, I wondered how a Protestant theology attentive to the body and its continual sensuous incursions into our thought might receive and engage this hermeneutical move. In what follows, I take up this task, first turning to Martin Luther, whose deep interest in a theology of creation was occluded by many of his modern readers with their single-minded focus on his theology of redemption. I then put him in conversation with Knut Løgstrup, whose attention to sensation invites a rich reclamation of the role of the body within Protestantism.

By way of a very rough summary, in what follows I will first articulate ways in which Luther understands the members of the body to function as signs of God. Next, I will consider Løgstrup's analysis of sensation, underscoring how his phenomenology of sensation allows us to see the body as that which has integrity, knows, and performs as body *per* se. This allows us to consider how the senses engage the cosmos, providing a promising possibility for a Protestant theology wanting to be attentive to creation and the body. In the final section of the paper, I will ponder how this promise of the senses is related to what I call the sense of promise: that capacity to encounter God in relationships with creation and the human creature, which is afforded all humans but revealed Christianly via word and sacrament.

Luther and the Song of Solomon

Oswald Bayer, has identified the theme of the promise as a *Grundton* in Luther's theology (Bayer, 2007: 29). As I explore this theme of the promise in relationship to our fleshly and sensual identity, I begin by considering some of Luther's comments on the Song of Solomon – an under-appreciated text of Luther's.

In considering Luther's treatment of this biblical book, it is first important to note that he considers this Song of Solomon to be an "encomium of the political order." (LW 15, 195) Any interest in reading it as a discourse on the relationship between God and the soul, as his forbearers did or in a more literal fashion, as some of our contemporaries do, are generally rejected. The book is about a people, not a person and follows after the tradition of the Song of Moses at the Red Sea. (LW 15, 192, 191) And yet, it would be a mistake to imagine that the text is reduced to some sort of a handbook on ruling. He notes that "the whole is as it were a conversation between God and His people, or between conscience and the Word." (LW 15, 213) The texts attends to the body politic and the body proper, both of which receive and make promises. Luther notes this theme of promise as he discusses the taking of an oath, raised in Song of Solomon 2:7. The text's "I adjure you, O daughters of Jerusalem, by the gazelles or the wild does" is considered an oath whereby these animals are taken to be surety for the promise made in the oath. Luther writes:

> First, then, these examples reveal that there is no simple prohibition against swearing. Secondly, there is sound enough reason to swear even by creatures when we advance them as signs of God, for that is not to make an idol out of a creature. (LW 15, 217)[3]

Luther's identification here of creatures as signs of God is not so very far from his assertion in the Genesis lectures that creatures—the sun, moon, heaven, earth, and humans—are words of God. (LW 1, 21) These "words" all speak of promise and an integrity is thereby accorded them, including the body, an important topic in the Song of Solomon.

Luther's engagement of this Song, with its heightened attentiveness to erotic imagery demands of him a kind of precision that he feels necessary for his readers. In reflecting on chapter 7, with its references to rounded thighs, navel, breasts, and neck, Luther notes that "even adolescents are capable of hearing and speaking about young women without concupiscence if they regard them as God's creation. … Accordingly He is here speaking about the genital members as about His own creation. … I say this so that no one will be offended by this text, which seems to be rather amatory." (LW 15, 249) Elsewhere he writes of women's bodily members as "good creatures of God." (LW 15, 231) And these creatures are good, above all else, because they are signs of God. These sorts of reflections are congruent with Luther's theological affirmation of the *finite capax infiniti*: the teaching that finite things can bear the infinite. This doctrinal affirmation of the fitness of created reality for the divine is supremely seen in the Incarnation, proximately evident in the Sacraments, yet widely assumed in the goodness of creation. The *capax*, however, did not received widespread approval during the Reformation, and many within the Protestant tradition reserve it for the Incarnation alone. Lutherans are Protestants

---

3 *Per se non peccatum, modo creaturam apprehendamus ut signum dei, qui se ostendit in ista creatura.* (WA-37, 651,7–8)

who affirm it more broadly, and it is for this reason that Luther can hold imagine the body to be a sign of God.

The personal and political body both, in part and in whole, function as signs pointing us to the divine promise. The body instantiates God's creative grace, which evokes faith to the end of divine-human intercourse. An important corollary of this is that the one who became flesh as the word incarnate is received in *carne*. Faith, for Luther, is a fleshly matter. But how about for modern Protestants? Can we hold forth such a possibility after Descartes? Here I turn to the Danish philosopher Knut Løgstrup to imagine a pathway forward for re-thinking the flesh in a contemporary context.

Løgstrup and Sensation

Løgstrup's philosophy of creation is deeply informed by an exploration of sensation, which is also used to tease out some contours for a theology of creation. At the heart of his philosophy is the foundational phenomenon of human beings as sensate. The very word "sensation" speaks to our primordial and perdurable experience of being in the world by means of encounters with what is sensible, and at the core of these events are their "absolutely independent" nature. (Løgstrup, 1995a: vii) In what follows I will explore this analytic of sensation considering it from the perspective of understanding, consciousness and art before engaging some relevant themes in theology proper in service of reclaiming the importance of the body for a contemporary Protestant theology.

Sensation, Understanding and Bodily Integrity

A fitting place to begin an exploration of Løgstrup's analysis of sensation is with his observation that we have become a-cosmic, imagining that we can think about the universe from outside of the world. (Løgstrup, 1995b: 43; Løgstrup, 1995a: 170) Løgstrup's protestation of this modern prejudice both provides an accounting of the genesis of this intellectual inheritance and a foundation for reforming thought about sensation proper, the latter being of especial importance to this essay.

Perhaps the most important point to be made is that in sensation, the human is distance-less. He also uses the word "omnipresent" to describe our sensation. In noting the relationship between sensation and understanding he writes:

> Nevertheless, sensation and understanding are opposed to each other and continue to be. Sensation lacks distance. The seen and heard are at a distance from our body but not at a distance from our sensation. The ship we see out on the ocean, the dog's bark

down in the village are far away from our body but not from our vision and hearing. Our understanding is the opposite. (Løgstrup, 1995b: 6)

Sensation knows no distance in that it is immediately attentive to the object of its sensing. The dog is now in my ear. The plane in the sky is now in my eye. There is no distance between my sensing and what I sense.[4] Sensing takes place in the mode of pure receptivity, and the knowledge of what was sensed that follows – as we begin to ponder what we have seen, heard, etc. – is what enables distance, which follows from what Løgstrup calls a "withdrawal." It is at this point – or rather in this existential of being human – that "we go from the level of sensing nature to the level of language-endowed nature." (Løgstrup, 1995b: 35) Understanding arrives as language makes possible the articulation of distance and so the knowledge both of something and of our sensation of it as first an experience of being sensed by the universe. (Løgstrup, 1995b: 20, 21) The universe is sensing us, and this is the condition for the possibility of our sensing.

Understanding works insofar as we stop seeing, hearing, tasting, smelling, feeling what we see, hear, taste, smell and feel, and think about these sensations. (Løgstrup, 1995a: 125) And so, while space is sensation's primary modality, time is the purview of understanding. (Løgstrup, 1995a: 123) And yet, the two are not unrelated, and the openness of space is the condition required for understanding to form. (Løgstrup, 1995a: 126) Understanding, however, does not free sensation *from* the universe which it senses, even while I can enjoy and engage the newly created distance between my ear and the flute at the front. But now space is created for interpretation etc. The senses, then, in their withdrawal create the condition for the possibility of understanding the universe that first senses us.

Sensations, above all else, as illumined by Løgstrup's phenomenology are marked by integrity. They have a kind of unity and coherence before understanding analyses them, as noted above in Løgstrup's description of them as "absolutely dependent." Our sensual capacities point to the honour accorded bodies, as bodies. It is not the case that we have bodies, as per some Cartesian dualism, but that we are bodies that first sense the cosmos. In the first instance then, the human is sensual and our sensation is integral to whom we are.

---

4 This calls to mind Luther's use of ubiquity, in a relative sense to describe voice and hearing in his treatment of the Eucharist, using the seeming fullness of voice to illustrate in an analogical fashion the manner in which omnipresence is not beyond the pale of our imagination.

Sensation, Technology and the Consciousness Body

Løgstrup notes that humans both live lives separated from the world and yet live "encapsulated" within it under the discipline of biological and medical sciences. (Løgstrup, 1995b: 9) We experience relative bondage and freedom with respect to the world in a knowledge shaped now by technology. Accordingly, either a kind of despair at our alienation—because of technology—or an overly confident trust in it obtains, that Løgstrup identifies with living at the edge of the natural world. In a fashion, we replace the omnipresence that is sensation for the "mastery" technology offers us at the supposed edge of reality—above the fray of the flesh; this distance is now the prized place for the technocrat.

Løgstrup notes that tools were once created to meet needs, but now the opposite is the case. (Løgstrup, 1995b: 46) Our dependence on technology has dulled our instincts. (Løgstrup, 1995b: 55) The use of instruments to extend the body has accompanied an increasingly instrumental view of the body. Accordingly, the spectre of thought as the apex of human value increases to the point that the category of "consciousness" is hereby restricted to thought alone. Løgstrup critiques this, noting that "consciousness" really refers to activities of both sensation and understanding. We are bodily conscious of what we sense and we are intellectually conscious of that experience in understanding it. Løgstrup notes our propensity to pretend that our intellective consciousness has an infinite capacity for understanding. (Løgstrup, 1995b: 28) Moreover, this becomes the only way we think about "consciousness," and it thereby too often replicates the dangers of Cartesian dualism and falls prey to obsessive self-reference. It is almost as if to be intellectually conscious is the core and sole determinant of being human. Indeed, he notes with some irony that a worldview in which sensation is ignored "can only be tested with the help of sensation." (Løgstrup, 1995b: 24) Sensation reminds us that our sensing occurs at the power of the universe; in this sense we are powerless (Løgstrup, 1995b: 28) even while this work of the universe on humans is not deemed to be a monism insofar as the universe intends us an actual "other" (Løgstrup, 1995b: 33) The universe presses upon us without our mastery of it, and yet it is not the case that this sensation is mere "fodder" for the understanding, which then makes sense of it. (Løgstrup, 1995a: 123) The universe is fully present to sensation and so a rich knowing occurs via the senses.

The body that has integrity is then also a knowing body. Of course, we experience this in mundane ways, in our flinching from discomfort or in experiencing muscle memory. The body sometimes knows things that are intellectually illusive. Instinct, which still accrues to us in some rudimentary fashions reminds us that there is a knowing that is proper to the body. Sometimes this knowing protests and sometimes it affirms what it encounters; we are mistaken to imagine that this sensual knowledge is somehow deficient. The body knows in the totality and integrity of its sensual consciousness what is sometimes lost in our slip into self-consciousness. We are bidden to listen to the body.

Sensation, Art and the Performing Body

In exploring the role of sensation in contemporary life Løgstrup has little confidence in science as an ally, noting its propensity to eliminate sensation and the everyday in seeking hidden causal explanations. Poetry, by contrast, is of great interest to him.

Art, with its attention to teleology and sensation is seen to be an important resource as a pathway to knowledge of the universe. He asserts in both *The Ethical Demand* and *Metaphysics* that poetry is an especially important genre of art to this end, noting how its use of indirect discourse gives it unique leverage in exploring what is overlooked. (Løgstrup, 1997: 197, 198; Løgstrup, 1995a: 42) It engages reason and reasons by bending grammar and by probing and evoking sensation. (Løgstrup, 1995b: 115) Sensation is aesthetically explored precisely because it is also aesthetically generative.

It seems that there is, then, a connection being made between art and sensation that presumes that the universe opens itself to the artist, who trades in the wares of deferral and indirect discourse. An opening to the mystery of being is facilitated by the unexpected, or perhaps unexplained and unexplainable sensations. At a fundamental level, it seems, that this makes sense. A constant noise becomes white noise; a familiar odor is taken for granted; a frequent sight becomes invisible. Artists are able to make these everyday revelations of being accessible to us. They do this by way of taking the ordinary and setting it askance or askew, just off what is expected in order to cause a second look, an extra hearing. Artists, it seems, take their cues from the senses—attentive to that which is ready to hand and pressing upon their curiosity that is evasive of ostensive explanations. And so, Løgstrup can claim that the "power to form a totality is only aesthetically accessible" (Løgstrup, 1995b: 73, 74) and yet in this same section he notes how the aesthetic move is ever and only evocative, symbolic in character and so drawing upon its participation in the universe even while recognizing that its temptation is to express unequivocally what avoids precisely this. And yet, the artist persists.

It might be helpful to consider Løgstrup's observations around art in light of an aesthetic actions closer to the body: such as dance, or perhaps some sports. Here the body responds to what it experiences, albeit in an indirect and so symbolic way. The body that is whole in its sensation and knows by way of interaction with the universe, is also a body that communicates what it experiences. The body, then, is performative. By performing its knowledge in space—here with a smile, there with a gesture—the body announces its place in the universe. The body is not only impressed in its sensation but expressive in its modality of reception.

Receiving the sunlight, or the song of a bird results in a bodily performance that communicates this experience to the world before a thought is ever formed, or a sentence constructed. The body that is whole knows the cosmos and expresses that knowledge in performance.

Sensation, the Body and Theology

The sensual body that is whole, knowing and performative offers clues for responding to ultimate questions. What contribution does the body make, then, to a theology attentive to creation as a peer of redemption? (Prenter, 1967: 200)

It is beyond the scope of this paper to address Løgstrup's theology of creation beyond a very view insights from this philosopher that bear upon the matter at hand. First, we should note that he thinks modern theologians who eschew a philosophical comprehensive horizon for their theology are mistaken if they think this propensity to dispense of philosophy comes from Luther. (Løgstrup, 1995a: 226) And yet he is also mindful, as a philosopher and a theologian, that any philosophy that attempts to sketch the contours of such a horizon imbibes hubris if it pretends that it can serve a programmatic function. A philosophy of creation (that which is constructed by a phenomenology of the sensations) is not to be equated with a theology of creation. (Løgstrup, 1995a: 278, 309; Gregersen, 2017: 61–63) The gospel announces what cannot be anticipated: God reigns by renouncing the divine's power of annihilation. (Løgstrup, 1995a: 310) And yet, following Grundtvig, he is able to see some coherence between philosophy and theology, between the law, which can be anticipated and is universal in nature, and the gospel, which is unexpected and particular in Christ. Both express God's power to make and keep promises, and do so with the capacity to enlighten the human. (Løgstrup, 1995a: 229) The God of promise wills the flourishing of the cosmos and the microcosmos, which is the human, including the body.

Philosophy and theology are both attentive to the human experience in all its complexity. He notes that experiences such as mysticism and esoteric religiosity open us to the "divine universe," but he is also aware that religious experience alone is insufficient, and so looks to doctrine as an interpretive key for integration. (Løgstrup, 1995a: 203) Doctrine, allows the individual to understand their experience under the tutelage of those who have reflected on their own in the school of experience that is theology. Here, we see that Løgstrup remains Protestant in the sense that the task of interpretation is perdurable, since the data for theological reflection is ever evolving, and so received hermeneutically. Sensation, for the Christian, is not to be understood in abstraction from theology but as an opening to reality that is rich for theological reflection.

Finally, we see then that body, complete with its sensual capacities, is rich with data for theological reflection. The sensual body that is whole, knowing and performative offers clues to ultimate questions, even if this data needs to be unpacked and interpreted with the aid of theological resources.

Conclusion

In conclusion, I hope to make a modest contribution to carnal hermeneutics, one informed by insights garnered from Luther and Løgstrup. In so doing, I want to put some flesh, as it were, on the phrase "the promise of the senses" and so provide an instance of a Protestant theology in a constructive modality. Such a theology is procedural rather than substantive in its assertion that this task of reading the body and thinking about what it tells us will never be complete.

It strikes me that Løgstrup's representation of the capacity of the human both to receive the universe in sensation and to discern it in the interplay between sensation and understanding is a rich theme, a theme further fueled when put alongside of Luther's claim in his treatment of the First Article in The Large Catechism:

> For here we see how the Father has given to us himself with all creation and has abundantly provided for us in this life, apart from the fact that he has also showered us with inexpressible eternal blessings through his Son and the Holy Spirit, as we shall hear. (Luther, 2000: 433)

Because God promises to be present to creation, and the cosmos is present to us in sensation, we discern via sensation the divine presence to us in our mode of pure receptivity. I name this the "sense of promise," drawing upon the objective genitive case, to underscore that sensation is able to discern a promise in the cosmos. Sensations discern God's presence in the universe. This is the promise of the senses. Yet the senses are also promising, in the subjective sense of the genitive case, insofar as they have the capacity to sense this presence of God. Perhaps we might name this promising ability that of intuiting the fullness of the universe in its mode of giving. The senses are promising because they sense promise. Løgstrup points to a kind of oscillation: sensation receives the universe in its pure receptivity and then receives the universe still further in the withdrawal that it undertakes from the universe in understanding. To exemplify: I stand before a tree with my hand on it: feeling the strong yet pliable bark, seeing the early summer light flicker through the leaves above me, smelling the pure air it offers, hearing the rustle of leaves. I almost identify with the tree, and then I step back and memories of other trees, of childhood come rushing in, along with images of clear cut forests and memories of the sour smell of pulp mills. And as understanding accrues with these memories—both pleasing and painful memories. I am reminded of the human condition in all of its complexity, and human life in its sovereign expressions—those spontaneous acts, characterized by openness that reflect human authenticity. (Løgstrup, 2007: 54–68) Alongside of these sovereign expressions of life, however, are their opposites. Yet these expressions of death are countered by both the universe's expansive character and the manner in which that same universe evokes and makes possible willing and doing that speak in sovereign expressions of life to a future beyond this present.

What then of people who live and have lived as Matthew, with a severe brain injury and unable to communicate in a conventional fashion? What promises do senses hold for those we know with like challenges? It seem that we can't ask them, but Laura, Matthew's mother, speaks of how she was able to discern traces as she read his body. She knew the integrity of his body, its capacity to know and its performative mode of being. She sensed his body enjoying certain phenomena and she felt its pain too. She perceived his body in modalities of both protestation and affirmation. She knows that there isn't only more here than what meets the eye; she also knows the eye meets more here than what we purport to know and so found in her son both the promise of the senses and a sense of promise. Someone like Matthew, then, speaks to us of the gift of the body and the power of the flesh, and in so doing, enables Protestants, and others, to find in the flesh an ally that keeps secularism honest and religion relevant.

Bibliography

Bayer, Oswald (2007). *Theology the Lutheran Way*. Translated by Jeffrey G. Silcock and Mark C. Mattes. Grand Rapids: Eerdmans.

Gregersen, Niels Henrik (2017). "K.E. Løgstrup and Scandinavian Creation Theology." In *Reformation Theology for a Post-Secular Age: Løgstrup, Prenter, Wingren, and the Future of Scandinavian Creation Theology*, edited by Niels Henrik Gregersen, Bengt Kristennson Uggla, and Trygve Wyller. Göttingen: Vandenhoek & Ruprecht.

Grosz, Elizabeth (1994). *Volatile Bodies: Toward a Corporeal Feminism*. Indianapolis: Indiana University Press.

Kearney, Richard (2015). "The Wager of Carnal Hermeneutics." In *Carnal Hermeneutics*, edited by Richard Kearney and Brian Treanor, 15–56. New York: Fordham University Press.

Løgstrup, Knud E. (1995a). *Metaphysics Volume I*. Translated by Russell L. Dees. Milwaukee: Marquette University Press.

Løgstrup, Knud E. (1995b). *Metaphysics Volume II*. Translated by Russell L. Dees. Milwaukee: Marquette University Press.

Løgstrup, Knud E. (1997). *The Ethical Demand*. Translated by T. Jensen, G. Puckering, and E. Watkins. Notre Dame, Ind.: University of Notre Dame Press, 1997.

Luther, Martin (1955–1986). *Luther's Works – American Edition*. Edited by Jaroslav Pelikan and H.T. Lehmann, 55 Volumes. Saint Louis and Philadelphia: Concordia and Fortress.

Luther, Martin (1914). *D. Martin Luthers Werke: Kritische Gesamtausgabe 31.2 Band*. Weimar: Hermann Böhler Nachfolger.

Luther, Martin (2000). "The Large Catechism." In *The Book of Concord: The Confessions of the Evangelical Lutheran Church*. Edited by Timothy J. Wengert and Robert Kolb. Minneapolis, MN: Fortress Press.

MacGregor, Geddes M. (1991). *Dictionary of Religion and Philosophy*. New York: Paragon House.

McClintock Fulkerson, Mary (1994). *Changing the Subject: Women's Discourse and Feminist Theology*. Minneapolis: Fortress Press.

Prenter, Regin (1967). *Creation and Redemption*. Translated by Theodor I Jensen. Philadelphia: Fortess Press.

Taylor, Charles (2007). *A Secular Age*. Cambridge, Mass.: Harvard University Press.

Taylor, Charles (1989). *Sources of the Self: The Making of the Modern Identity*. Cambridge: Harvard University Press.

Taylor, Charles (1991). The Malaise of Modernity. Toronto: Anansi Press, 1991.

Index

art   129
baptism   10–11, 38, 60–62, 74–75, 80, 87, 90–91, 93, 95
Berger, Peter   12, 32, 42, 70, 75–76, 80, 84, 99
body   35, 59–60, 117, 122–131
Christianism   111–112, 118–119
Church of Norway   83–85, 87–93, 96, 112
Circumcision   14, 51–63, 67–81
cultural heritage   84, 94–98, 100
dimensions of Protestantism   11, 83, 93
discursive field   86, 100, 104, 106
Faith-based migration practices   112–113, 118
formatting   12–14, 17–19, 23–25, 67, 69, 71–73, 75, 79–81, 84, 92, 94
health service   57, 68, 78
humanistic Islam   18, 23, 25–27
Islam   14, 17–27, 40–41, 45, 59, 79–80, 83–84, 87, 92, 98, 104–105
Islamic university theology   23–25
Judaism   18, 52, 57, 67–69, 71–76, 78, 80
law   11, 18–19, 27, 36, 51–63, 68–70, 73, 84–85, 92, 94–95, 98, 106, 112–113, 116, 118, 130
Luther, Martin   20, 22, 122–126, 131

Løgstrup, Knud Eiler   115, 121–132
masculinity   60–62
media texts   67, 69–71, 79–80
nones   83–87, 90–93, 96, 99, 104–106
non-religion   62, 83, 85–90, 93–94, 98–100, 105–106
Oslo   71, 83–94, 97, 99, 104–106
Pentecostalisation   35–45
Pentecostalism   10, 12, 31–46, 74–76, 80
Procedural ethics   115–118
Protestant ethic   9, 18, 31–32, 42, 114–118
Protestant Islam   17–21
Protestantisation   11–13, 18–19, 31, 35–37, 67–73, 77–80, 84–85, 91, 93, 106
religious motivation   52, 56–57, 60–62
Roy, Oliver   13, 14, 17–24, 84, 92, 98
Scandinavian creation theology   14, 111–112, 118, 122
self-formatting   18–19, 23–25, 27
sensation   124, 126–131
sign and signified   59, 73–75, 80
Taylor, Charles   96, 105, 123
traveling theory   17, 19
Weber, Max   9, 11, 22–23, 31–32, 34–35, 42–43, 114–116

Notes on Contributors

Erlend Hovdkinn From is a Doctoral candidate at The Faculty of Theology, University of Oslo. His main area of research is Sociology of (non)religion. Relevant publication: From, E.H. (2022). "State and (Non)religion: Perspectives from Nones in Oslo" in: Zwilling, A-L., Årsheim, H. (eds.) Nonreligion in Late Modern Societies. Institutional and Legal Perspectives. Springer, Cham. https://doi.org/10.1007/978-3-030-92395-2_10

Vebjørn Horsfjord is professor of religion and ethics at Inland Norway University of Applied Sciences. His main research interests are interreligious studies, religion and human rights, and world Christianity with a focus on the Orthodox tradition. His PhD (2015) was on Muslim – Christian dialogue. He has published i.a. Common Words in Muslim – Christian Dialogue (Brill, 2017) and co-authored Global Christianity – Current trends (Pickwick publications, 2022).

Allen Jorgenson is Assistant Dean at Martin Luther University College at Wilfrid Laurier University in Waterloo Ontario, where he holds the William D. Huras Chair in Ecclesiology and Church History. His research areas include Martin Luther, Friedrich Schleiermacher and comparative theology. His recent publications include Indigenous and Christian Perspectives in Dialogue (Lexington, 2021) and a volume he co-edited with Kris Kvam entitled The Crux of Theology: Martin Luther's Teachings and Our Work for Freedom, Justice, and Peace (Lexington/Fortress Press, 2022).

Oddbjørn Leirvik is professor emeritus at The Faculty of Theology, University of Oslo. His research areas include Islam and Christian Muslim relations, systematic theology and interfaith dialogue. Relevant publication: "Interreligious Studies. A Relational Approach to Religious Activism and the Study of Religion" (Bloomsbury, 2014).

Gina Lende is an associate professor in religious studies at MF Norwegian School for Theology, Religion and Society. Her research areas include contemporary Islam and Christianity and its political and public role. She is the co-author of the book *Global Christianity – current trends and developments*, Pickwick Publications (2022).

Karin Neutel is a lecturer at Umeå University, Sweden. Her research areas include Biblical Studies, with a focus on contemporary social and political uses of the Bible. Relevant publications: Karin B. Neutel, "The Bible in Migration Politics in Northern Europe", *Svensk Exegetisk Årsbok* 87, 2022. Karin B. Neutel and Marianne Bjelland Kartzow, "'God Speaks Our Language': Recent Scandinavian Bible Translations and the Heritagization of Christianity" in Marianne Bjelland Kartzow, Outi Lehtipuu and Kasper Bro Larsen (eds.), *The Nordic Bible* (Berlin: De Gruyter, 2022).

Tarald Rasmussen is professor emeritus of Church History at The Faculty of Theology, University of Oslo. His primary research area is the history of early modern Christianity, especially in Germany and the Nordic countries. Recent publications include "Monastic Life and Monastic Theology in Early Modern Germany" in: David Whitford (ed.): *Martin Luther in Context*, Oxford UP 2018 "Remembering the Past in the Nordic Reformations", in: Cummings, Law, Riley and Walsham: *Remembering the Reformation*, Routledge 2020 and "Ambiguous Memories of the Reformation – The Case of Norway", In: *Journal of Early Modern Christianity* Vol. 7, Issue 2 (2020).

Trygve Wyller is professor emeritus at The Faculty of Theology, University of Oslo. His main areas of research include theologies and ethics of Christian social practice (diaconia), migration and space studies, phenomenology and theology and re-interpretations of Scandinavian Creation Theology. Some recent publications: Wyller, T (2022). "Diaconia / Empowering / Social Development" in: *International Handbook of Practical Theology* (Ed. Weyel, B, Gräb, W, Lartey, W, Wepener, C). Berlin: De Gruyter. Wyller, T (2021). "The sensory and the heterotopic. Traces of a decentering ecclesiology", in: Roth, U, Gilly, A (Hrsg.) *Die Religiöse Positionierung der Dinge. Zur Materialität und Performativituät religiöser Praxis*. Stuttgart: Kohlhammer 2021.

Vegard Ree Ytterbøe, Research assistant, Church History, Faculty of Theology at the University of Oslo. Primary field of research: Law and religion in early modern and modern Scandinavia. He has written a master's thesis on blasphemy laws in Norway in the first half of the 19th century.